# EDUCATION & Anarchy

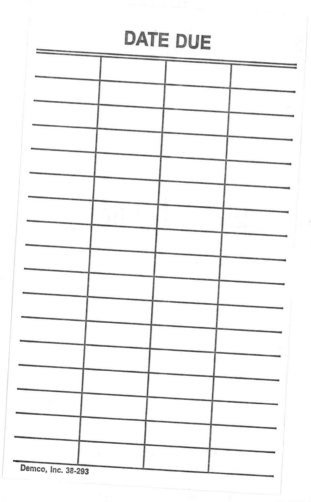

**Copyright © 2001 by**
**University Press of America,® Inc.**
4720 Boston Way
Lanham, Maryland 20706

12 Hid's Copse Rd.
Cumnor Hill, Oxford OX2 9JJ

**Library of Congress Cataloging-in-Publication Data**

Engel, Bill.
Education & anarchy / Bill Engel.
p.   cm
The A in anarchy is circled which represents the anarchy symbol.
Includes bibliographical references (p.).
l. Memory. 2. Learning. I. Title: Education and anarchy. II. Title.
LB1063 .E42 2001   370.15'2—dc21   2001031536 CIP

ISBN 0-7618-2052-5 (pbk. : alk. paper)

⊖™ The paper used in this publication meets the minimum
requirements of American National Standard for Information
Sciences—Permanence of Paper for Printed Library Materials,
ANSI Z39.48—1984

For Fred Key,
*whose capers were always elegant and error-free.*

We are on our way to . . . "a revolution by due course of law." This is undoubtedly,—if we are still to live and grow, and this famous nation is not to stagnate and dwindle away on the one hand, or, on the other, to perish miserably in mere anarchy and confusion,—what we are on the way to. Great changes there must be, for a revolution cannot accomplish itself without great changes; yet order there must be, for without order a revolution cannot accomplish itself by due course of law. So whatever brings risk of tumult and disorder . . . our best self, or right reason, plainly enjoins us to set our faces against.

—Matthew Arnold, *Culture and Anarchy* (1869/1961: 444)

*The power to think* and *the desire to rebel.* These faculties, combining their progressive action in history, represent the essential factor, the negative power in the positive development of human animality, and create consequently all that constitutes humanity in man. . . . Three elements or, if you like, three fundamental principles constitute the essential conditions of all human development, collective or individual, in history: (1) human *animality*; (2) *thought*; and (3) *rebellion*. To the first properly corresponds *social and private economy*; to the second, *science*; to the third, *liberty*.

—Michael A. Bakunin, *God and the State* (1871/1970: 9, 12)

Would life, with all its inevitable drudgery and sorrows, be worth living if, besides daily work, man could never obtain a single pleasure according to his individual tastes? . . . After bread has been secured, leisure is the supreme aim. . . . And as all men do not and cannot resemble one another (the variety of tastes and needs is the chief guarantee of human progress) there will always be, men and women whose desire will go beyond those of ordinary individuals in some particular direction. . . . Some like statues, some pictures. A particular individual has no other ambition than to possess a good piano, while another is pleased with an accordion. The tastes vary, but the artistic needs exist in all. . . . But as we must recognize that man has other needs besides food, and as the strength of anarchy lies precisely in that it understands *all* human faculties and *all* passions, and ignores none, we shall, in a few words, explain how man can contrive to satisfy all his intellectual and artistic needs.

—Peter Kropotkin, *Conquest of Bread* (1892/1995: 94-96)

# Contents

Figures     vii
Acknowledgments     ix
Preface     xi

Introduction     1

**1. Classroom Capers**     21
    I.   Grounding     21
    II.   Five Main Types     49
      1.   Tagging     49
      2.   Memory Grids     54
      3.   Mind Mapping     56
      4.   Magic Circles     62
      5.   Speaking Pictures     66
    III. Moving On     74

**2. Letting Learning Happen**     75
    I.   Manifesto     75
    II.   Demonstration     79
      1.   Plan of Study     91
        1st Unit: Macrocosm & Microcosm     92
        2nd Unit: Discovery of the Self     92
        3rd Unit: The Will to Power     92
        4th Unit: World of Words     92
      2. Motto, Expectations, and Key Questions     93
    III. Credo     95

**3.  Speaking of Teaching**                                          99

**4.  What Can Be Taught**                                           127
   I.  Preamble                                        127
   II.  Three Possibilities                            131
      1.  Literature and Human Values    134
      2.  Educating the Princes          135
      3.  Books with Bill                137
   III. Drawing the Line                               144

**5.  The Sword of Truth**                                           147
   I.  Introduction                                    147
   II.  The Way of the Sword                           150
      1.  Salute                         154
      2.  On Guard                       155
      3.  Preparations                   156
        • Body Movements        157
        • Blade Actions         160
      4.  Offensive                      162
        • Attacks               164
        • Ripostes              164
        • Varied Offensive      166
      5.  Defensive                      166
        • Evasions              166
        • Parries               168
      6.  Counter Offensive              170
   III. Lessons Learned from Fencing                    170

Conclusion                                                           177

Bibliography                                                         179

Book at a Glance                                                     187

About the Author                                                     189

# Figures

0.1. The New Cerberus (adapted from Selman et al., 1998)   9
0.2. Map of the Book   15

1.1. Repeated Caper, "Personalized Epistemeter"   24
1.2. Chaistic Map of *Paradise Lost* (adapted from Crump, 1976)   30
1.3. *Beowulf* Caper Sheet
(Survey of English Literature, Harriet Goodrich)   32
1.4. Mnemic-bites (Survey of English Literature, Kristin West)   34
1.5. Three Vignettes in *Beowulf*, Fitt 9
(Survey of English Literature, Paul Richter)   36
1.6. Graphic Flow-Chart of Sackville's "Induction"
to *The Mirror For Magistrates*   37
1.7. Moral Topography of Dante's *Inferno*
(Barry Moser's drawing; Mandelbaum, 1988)   40
1.8. Frontispiece to Lodge's *Works of Seneca*
(early seventeenth century)   41
1.9. Frontispiece to Ralegh's *History of the World* (1614)   42
1.10. Frontispiece to Burton's *Anatomy of Melancholy* (1660)   43
1.11. *Impresa* for Today
(Survey of English Literature, Caroline Worrell)   45
1.12. Map of Bacon's "On Death"
(Seventeenth Century course, Rico Blancaflor)   46
1.13. Five Main Types of Mnemonic Capers   50
1.14. Tagging, key words in Chaucer's *Canterbury Tales*,
"General Prologue"   53
1.15. Tagging, bare bones for a Memory Grid
(Renaissance Drama, Shalani Goel)   55

1.16. Memory Grid
(Survey of English Literature, Kara McKenney) 57
1.17. Mind Map, characters encountered in *Everyman* 58
1.18. Mind Map, moral points in Skelton's *Bouge of Court*
(Sixteenth Century course, Emily Gross) 59
1.19. Mind Map, Spenser's *Faerie Queene*, II.12
(Sixteenth Century course, Bryan Power) 61
1.20. Mind Map, Burton's *Anatomy*, III.4.2.6
(Seventeenth Century course, Rico Blancaflor) 62
1.21. Magic Circle, tally sheet (Introduction to Poetry) 63
1.22. Magic Circle, template (Introduction to Poetry) 64
1.23. Memory Grid, Kerouac's *On the Road*
(Freshman Seminar: Life as Journey) 65
1.24. Magic Circle, course outline
(Freshman Seminar: Life as Journey) 66
1.25. Speaking Picture, course outline (Great Books) 68
1.26. Speaking Picture, mnemonic itinerary
(Survey of English Literature, Britt Farwick) 71
1.27. Speaking Picture, acrostic mnemonic tagging
(Survey of English Literature, Kelly West) 72
1.28. Speaking Picture, visual epitome
(Survey of English Literature, Shawn Baldwin) 73

2.1. Mnemonic Learning Pyramid—View from Above 80
2.2. Chart showing "A Series of Useful Correspondences" 81
2.3. Mind-Map of Pico's *Oration on the Dignity of Man*
(NEH/CBE seminar, Dede Clements) 86
2.4. Pyramid of Studies 87
2.5. Commonplace book, Vitruvian Man to show Pico's ideas
(NEH/CBE seminar, Cal Fuller) 89
2.6. Commonplace Book, Vitruvian Man to show authors'
ideas (NEH/CBE seminar, Cal Fuller) 90

4.1. Schooling—at a glance 132
4.2. Education—at a glance 133

5.1. Preparations, options chart (with permission, USFA) 158
5.2. Offensive, options chart (with permission, USFA) 165
5.3. Defensive, options chart (with permission, USFA) 167
5.4. Counter-Offensive, options chart (with permission, USFA) 171

# Acknowledgments

I am indebted primarily to students I have encountered, especially those who actively helped me explore alternative approaches to learning and grading, when I was at the University of Pennsylvania, Jon Pochos, Robin Nielsen, and Scott Strauss; at the University of California at Berkeley, Joel Nevins, Anya Neher, and Scott Robertson; and, at Vanderbilt University, Frank Bass, Andrea Becksvoort, Dierks Bentley, Rico Blancaflor, John Chiappetta, Gene Cook, Edourd Corso, David Coviello, Mary Curry, Olivia Daane, John Deboben, Heather Delio, Andrew DeSimone, Kara Dinardo, Britton Dubina, Doug Eure, Will Fisher, Anil Gocklani, Shalani Goel, Andy Grogan, Clay Hensley, Michael Hillegass, Eliot Houser, Kelley Kitchens, Michelle Lokey, Taylor Mayes, Kelly McGregor, Kelly Mullins, Maurie Nicely, Tom Noser, David Nuss, Matt Oles, Conoley Ospovat, Joy Phillips, Todd Piccirilli, David Rushton, Craig Spengler, Adriane Stewart, and Martin Wilson.

I owe thanks to Israel Scheffler and Vernon Howard of the Philosophy of Education Research Center at Harvard University where I was a Visiting Scholar when this project first took shape; to the Academy for Creative Teaching for giving me opportunities to report on what I was learning in the field; and to the United States Fencing Association, especially for permission to reproduce the diagrams in Chapter 5. Doug Harris, a truly great coach: thanks.

Teachers, colleagues, and friends who have commented on this book from the start include Emerson Brown, Andrew Krichels, LeBaron Moseby, Bud Schultz, and Ken Simon. Miriam Halachmi has helped me to recognize the need for balancing the "Pedagogy of Punishment and Consequences" with the "Pedagogy of Permission and Self Reliance" (the latter which, it is no secret, I prefer). Hans Klein has kept faith with me from the first time I put pen to paper about teaching. Cal Fuller lent a critical eye to the manuscript before it went to press, and Dorothy Albritton has helped to make this book a delight for readers to take in hand.

Parts of this book have been presented at conferences and published in scholarly journals. Chapter 1 grew out of "The Aesthetic Core of Memory Training," *Creative Teaching* 1 (1998), 91-111; subsequent developments of my theme are scheduled appear as "Being Mindful of Memory's Lessons," *Midwest Philosophy of Education Proceedings* (1999/2000) and as "The Case for Using Mnemonics," *Connotations* 9.2 (2001). Chapter 2 was the result of my working with teachers at Montgomery Bell Academy as part of a Council for Basic Education (NEH) Summer Humanities Seminar; the ensuing research was presented at a plenary session of the International Council for Innovation in Higher Education at National University in 1998. Also, the "Credo" at the end of Chapter 2 was presented in earlier forms as a seminar paper at the Association for Core Texts and Courses in 1999, and as a lecture hosted by the Honor's Program at the University of Alabama in Birmingham in 2000. Chapter 3 grew out of a workshop sponsored by the Tennessee Arts Academy hosted by Belmont University in 1998; and a panel at the Midwest Philosophy of Education Meeting in November 1999 (a version is to be published in the *MPES Proceedings*, which was vastly improved by a lucid summation of my work in pragmatic aesthetics offered by Michael Schwartz, and also by critical suggestions facilitated by Nicholas C. Burbules at *Educational Theory*). Chapter 4 is based on "Can Ethics Be Taught? To Lawyers?" *Creative Teaching* 2 (1999), 77-84; and some of the ideas subsequently were field-tested in "Ethics and Professionalism" courses monitored by the Tennessee Commission on Legal Education. An earlier version of Chapter 5 was published as "The Way of the Sword: Lessons Learned from Fencing," *Creative Teaching* 3 (2000), 49-61. Heartfelt thanks go to Hans Klein and Denise Smith for editorial assistance on, and permission to use, aspects of my work that previously appeared in *Creative Teaching*. Finally, thanks go to Kaaren, Zoe, Simon, and Iris—you make it all worthwhile.

# Preface

## Introduction

Whatever job description, array of tasks, or mission a teacher sees as primarily defining his or her role as an educator, one thread runs through them all: Teachers can turn a form of chaos into a kind of order. Every teacher's nightmare is losing control of the class. Until you become aware of the extent to which this understanding informs your approach to education, your day-to-day decisions in the classroom will remain reactive in nature. And yet, anarchy dances hand in hand with education if learning is destined to occur. No matter how much it may be feared, or the lengths to which people go to short-circuit it, anarchy remains a vital, if unspoken, component—and is perhaps the motivating factor—of lasting learning.

The overarching theme lending coherence to **EDUCATION &** *Anarchy* is revolution. Revolution need not be construed politically or socially, although it often is. Revolution also names the cycle of return in nature that characterizes everything from the motion of heavenly bodies to the work of seeds. Also woodland animals, for example, shed their pelts to make way for new and more lustrous coats appropriate to the oncoming season. So too the cases and conditions covered in this book concern how we go about, or resist, shedding what is no longer needed or useful. All of the signs around me indicate that the season for change in education is upon us once again.

## Chapter 1: Classroom Capers

Visual memory cues and related mental triggering devices are as old as recorded history. Closer scrutiny of the main metaphors used to express such cues will help bring into focus the principles informing and animating an immemorial, if tacit, philosophy of education. This chapter traces the main contours of those principles and suggests that once they are recovered and judiciously adapted for contemporary classroom use, they can enable students to develop and cultivate luminous and often indelible points of connection to the material being studied. Specifically, five main types of mnemonic techniques are identified (Tagging, Memory Grids, Mind-Mapping, Magic Circles, and Speaking Pictures) and then used to illustrate the construction of study guides and learning aids, which collectively I call "capers." These capers are an integral part of students' portfolios and, taken together, chart visible stages in a student's ongoing journey toward knowledge. Capers help students become more responsible for what they are learning, and thus become more cognizant of the aesthetic core of what they have learned and more reflective about how this learning took place.

## Chapter 2: Letting Learning Happen

As in-service workshops and continuing education programs are fast becoming an indispensable part of the professional life of teachers today, we need to attend more closely to how we can "let learning happen." This chapter explores strategies that enable teachers once again to become students themselves in ways which honor their years of service and which respect their status as seasoned curriculum designers and effective classroom leaders. Some of the specific tactics used, while employed in the context of teaching intellectual history, are discussed with an eye toward encouraging you to contour them to fit your own prospective needs.

## Chapter 3: Speaking of Teaching

The central chapter exposes the predominantly verbal way we come to terms with art; and, by extension, with other closely related domains of inquiry and endeavor, like philosophy and like education. While paying tribute to how this issue traditionally has been cast, this chapter critically examines the implied end of art as discussed by Martin Heidegger and John Dewey. Although their writings on the distinctions between the aesthetic experience and the work of art appear at roughly the same time, neither sought to engage the findings of the other. Despite this, and notwithstanding the overwhelming political rift between Germany and America in the 1930's, their influential conclusions about the power of art and education to affect social change are remarkably similar.

My approach thus affords an unlooked for glimpse into the possibility that the making of art is the happening of truth. To flesh this out further—and to do so in a way that is consistent with, and disclosive of, the theme in question—this chapter is extraordinarily careful in its precise use of words. Also, by using self-conscious repetition, this chapter seeks to turn the tables on a dominant (and predominating) view of pragmatic aesthetics that (1) focuses on products and measurable outcomes to validate and verify artistic activity, and (2) is superficial in its conception of truth as being causal, consequential, and essentially mimetic. Accordingly this chapter argues, in a way that intentionally sidetracks the train of thought traditionally associated with logical positivism and pragmatic aesthetics, that (1) process needs to be balanced into the equation of assessing the full and true value of the work of art, and (2) truth hides itself most elusively in the folds of fair approximations and faithful representations of whatever is put forward as being the standard which, we are told by experts and public opinion alike, we should be seeking to copy, reproduce, and imitate.

## Chapter 4: What Can Be Taught

Continuing education programs and Internet based course-work have led to an extension and redefinition of the goals and needs of students. The resulting, more fluid, population of students has led educators to reconsider the limits of traditional instructional venues, as well as of what can be taught in the context of any prescribed course of study. It has also led to a general reassessment of how we go about delivering the material that is deemed important to be learned, irrespective of how this decision gets legislated and monitored. Even as we strive to keep abreast of these changes, we need to reflect on our roles as educators—especially our responsibilities to individual students.

Although the cases surveyed come primarily from my experiences as a provider of continuing legal education, in which works of literature are used to satisfy and to incite further the desire for life-long learning, this chapter raises broader questions that stem from a critical distinction between schooling and education. Many students look forward to continuing and, in some cases, finally enjoying their education only once they have left formal schooling. This chapter advocates that we work creatively with, and from within, the limits of what we think can be taught.

## Chapter 5: The Sword of Truth

To what extent does a student need a teacher to learn how to learn? Athletics in general, and fencing in particular, give us a handy way to explore the ramifications of this question. With fencing, as with any discipline, once basic skills are covered, learning is enhanced by drill and application. Answers come swiftly through practical action, for only what works in the field counts. Still, aesthetic and ethical considerations ensure that interaction among fencers remains equitable and elegant. Fencing brings into focus what otherwise might remain outside our field of vision by showing us "in other words" what our role might be toward those we seek to educate.

## Conclusion

Students must come first. If we are driven by anything else, then we are compromising what matters most in education. Teachers have much to learn; not only with respect to the content of what they teach, but also regarding how they are going teach it—this time. Each student provides you, the teacher, with opportunities to learn how you learn best. In this respect, teachers need to recognize they are students too. Education is about letting learning happen. More specifically, because the student comes first: education is about letting students learn. Despite pressures from above and from below, teachers are the first and last guardians of this truth.

# Introduction

It is more of a job to interpret the interpretation than to interpret the things, and there are more books about books than about any other subject: we do nothing but write glosses about each other. . . . Is it not the chief and most reputed learning of our times to learn to understand the learned? Is that not the common and ultimate end of all studies?

—Montaigne's *Essays*, III.13: 818

A principal motive for writing this book grew out of my admiration for the many and various studies published recently on topics relating to education and innovative pedagogy. Some were full of graphs and percentages and findings and theories; many had boxes and diagrams and inventories; some relied on anecdotal narratives of beleaguered teachers, others included articulate testimonials of the success (or failure) of this or that curriculum breakthrough, new way of assessing learning, or sure-fire way of getting in touch with different types of learners. Notwithstanding the usefulness and popularity of these studies though, many of which have reached millions of readers, I saw a need for a book that looked to some prior questions.

Specifically, I wanted to focus on the kinds of questions that precede setting up test groups; questions that come before the postulation of breakthroughs; questions that need to be asked before we can claim a revolution is, or is not, sweeping the American education scene today whether inside or outside the classroom. For, as Peter Kropotkin phrased it so sensibly in two articles that question how change comes about: "We must endeavor to discover and to enunciate in plain words the hopes, the faint, indistinct ideal which sets the masses in motion. The better understood, the more warmly taken to heart, the greater will be the results achieved, and less numerous the useless victims. . . . [The coming revolution] must grow naturally, proceeding from the simplest up to complex federations; and it cannot be something schemed by a few men and ordered from above" (Kropotkin, 1886-1907/1988: 22, 26). As I see it, to use Kropotkin's urgent rhetoric, among the numerous useless victims on the American educational scene are, first and foremost, students. By the same token, casualties also include those substitute teachers and adjuncts who would prefer full-time employment in the field of education. And then there are the administrators who find themselves in legislative double binds, trying to satisfy numerous, often competing, constituencies. Victims also include those people further up the chain of command who, in the interest of just keeping the machine rolling and keeping their posts secure, have done just that (Solomon and Solomon, 1993). Although the melancholy themes of loss, of unnecessary casualties, and of often unconscious victimization, are implicit in my book, I did not see the need to belabor the obvious point that human dignity, at times, is compromised in the name of classroom management and program implementation. Instead I have sought to speak plainly, and from experience, about what I take to be the "indistinct ideal which sets the masses in motion."

This book therefore speaks to that part of us which, at some point, has been unable to deny the unforeseen and often disruptive currents of chance, even discord, that end up shaping our everyday experiences of teaching and learning. And so this book grew out of my need to express (and in expressing, to find a new understanding of my relation to) the degree of control that we imagine we have over, say, the material being studied or which we have set out to teach; the control we imagine we have over supervisors or over students; control over the books we read or over those we write.

I am hardly alone in recognizing that the unrelenting urge to control rarely achieves anything of lasting merit, and often saps the joy out of the endeavor. By the same token, a teacher's satisfaction with packaging up and flawlessly delivering a lesson is at best illusory and at worst antithetical to open inquiry. What then can we do in the face of chaos, which, whether we acknowledge it or not, animates and drives our relation to learning and teaching? **EDUCATION &** *Anarchy* takes this question as its guiding premise.

Specifically, the first chapter, "Classroom Capers," examines techniques for tapping into and rechanneling typical educational anarchy by drawing on the Art of Memory, which I have revived from classical pedagogy and adapted for contemporary classroom use. Chapter 1 models a variety of ways this can be put into practice, and thus initiates an approach to questioning that many teachers recognize needs to be learned—or, more properly, relearned as it involves a kind of thinking that is really rethinking (Freire and Faundez, 1989: 35). It occurred to me that there are plenty of educators who, like me, are seeking to engage in a kind of questioning that goes back to the bedrock of what daily we take for granted. Learning questioning is a start. This is the foundation of my discussion, in Chapter 2, about how we can participate deliberately and reflectively in the process by which we let learning happen. And yet even when we find ourselves responding to this call, we tend do so verbally, notwithstanding our best intentions to use others mediums as well. Chapter 3 then, "Speaking of Teaching," shines a light on how words and other predominantly linear, cause-and-effect, approaches to learning tend to predestine and delimit our engagement with education. With this in mind, the kinds of rethinking and questioning discussed in this book involve cyclic forms of reflection and projection aimed at transformation. For example, as the next chapter "What Can Be Taught" goes on to consider, many students look forward to continuing and, in some cases, finally getting around to enjoying their education only once they have left formal schooling. Chapter 4 advocates that we work creatively with, and from within, the limits of what can be taught. But how are these limits realized? Taking this question to heart, Chapter 5, "The Sword of Truth," explores the extent to which a student needs a teacher to learn.

Given the methods and goals just described for each chapter, it will come as little surprise that the overarching theme lending coherence to **EDUCATION &** *(A)narchy* is revolution. Revolution need not be construed politically or socially, although it often is. Revolution also names the cycle of return in nature that characterizes everything from the motion of heavenly bodies to the work of seeds. Also woodland animals, for example, shed their pelts to make way for new and more lustrous coats appropriate to the oncoming season. So too the cases and conditions covered in this book concern how we go about, or resist, shedding what is no longer needed or useful. All of the signs around me indicate that the season for change in education is upon us once again.

In the spirit of cyclic return just mentioned, I would invite you to look back to the epigraph page, for it embodies and expresses what I take to be the main thematic concerns of **EDUCATION &** *(A)narchy*.

Among other things, this book advances the view that repetition—realized as repeated and active engagement with what is already at hand—makes for lasting learning. Repetition can make for lasting learning, however, only if there is a purpose to the repetition which marks it as being an experience that manifestly allows students to build on what they already know. This perennial touchstone concerning the value of repetition in learning is one that I seek to revive for our own day.

A century ago, in his preface to *The History of Xerxes*, Jacob Abbott wrote about the importance of acquiring sufficient preliminary knowledge to understand and appreciate "so condensed a generalization as a summary of the whole history of a nation contained in an ordinary volume." His conclusion is compelling, and it can be seen to link all five chapters of this book which promote "capers," or interactive memory-based exercises, as an antidote to a mind-numbing approach to teaching driven primarily by outcomes: "Without this degree of maturity of mind, and this preparation, the study of such a work will be, as it too frequently is, a mere mechanical committing to memory of names, and dates, and phrases, which awaken no interest, communicate no ideas, and impart no useful knowledge to the mind" (Abbott, n.d.: 5). If ever it was appropriate to quote the old adage, it is now: The more things change, the more they are the same.

Among the other views that I want to bring back and re-examine in a fresh light is the commonplace of student-life, and I believe of humanity in general, that the more decisions and rules are imposed from the top-down, the greater the pressure build-up from below. Often this has disastrous results since those who feel it most immediately tend to strike out at whatever is within immediate reach. All too often what ends up getting damaged is the one striking out, or those close to her or him, or property that is only symbolically connected to the cause of one's frustration at feeling powerless (McLeod, 1987). If my research had concerned violence in our schools, then this would have been the place for me to introduce a plan for defusing and transforming that rage; but as my training resides elsewhere, for now, I would invite those of you who are in closer contact with it than I am, to pick up this theme and carry it toward viable conclusions of your own.

For the purpose of this present study though, it will suffice for me to observe that administrators do a great disservice to everyone involved when they assume that students will not notice, or care, they are being left out of the decision-making process. Even more egregious is it when team leaders, chairs, or administrators think that forms of token representation (like letting students sit on certain committees, or like agreeing to hear a designated spokesman from a group with a grievance) will satisfy the call for more involvement in the decision-making process whether on the part of students or teachers. Such shows of concern are merely that—shows. While teachers may be more willing to go along with the show since their jobs and livelihood often are on the line, students are quick to note when they are being duped, though nowadays they are less likely to say anything about it. What they do about it though is what separates effective social change from the exacerbation and perpetuation of an untenable situation (Alinksy, 1972).

**EDUCATION &** *Anarchy* seeks to make just such an intervention in the process by providing a series of reflections and suggestions and projections. Far from advocating that we scorn or disregard what procedures and political realities we find already in place, we must take them as our ground zero and be familiar with them thoroughly so that we can ask tough questions and determine the best course of action—whether reform, replacement, or eradication (Goodman, 1964). **EDUCATION &** *Anarchy* is designed to encourage you to continue thinking critically, and to do so from a variety of perspectives, about how you have been educated and about how you tend to teach lessons to others (whether or not in a classroom), and how daily you are being educated by others— and this last point includes how you are being administrated, as well as the ways you have been rewarded, punished, or ignored for your performance and views.

Bud Schultz recalls a teacher at Trinity College who was denied reappointment at his departmental evaluation because the tenured faculty complained he "did not direct class discussion enough" and "did not test students enough." Obviously some standard of supervisory adequacy was assumed and found wanting (he was not doing "enough"). But what comes through even more clearly from this justification for his dismissal is the power of the unstated institutional definition of a teacher as a director; and further, the consequences of what happens when one doesn't (or won't) play the role as expected. The idea that students could accomplish something of worth while pursuing their own goals, and as it happened during the course of class discussion, cuts against the grain of traditional definitions of student and teacher roles—and thus is deemed intolerable. Sincerely to raise the question of what makes a teacher a teacher is tantamount to challenging what has come to operate as the rules that ultimately govern the fates of teacher and student alike. And so to ask what makes a teacher a teacher is perhaps a more radical inquiry than originally was supposed.

There seems to be a ubiquitous, apparently incontestable assumption that what it means to be an effective teacher is to have students score better than average on a test of one sort or another, whether a final exam or a nationally recognized "blacken in the bubble" standardized test (Ohanian, 1999). Once that assumption is granted, as it universally seems to be, the teacher becomes the director of students only to be directed herself by a supervisory body quite distant from the classroom. These sorts of issues give a concrete embodiment to the anarchy which some feel must constantly be checked, contained, and squelched. Still though, even if we want to think in a sustained and critical way about such issues, often we cannot start the process because we get so caught up with, and can become so engaged in, our duties associated with crowd-control and accountability, let alone managing our lives outside the workplace. And when you are connected to a school or institution—whether as a teacher or student—your activities might well include organizing the work of others, administrating programs, forming and being assigned to committees, attending meetings . . . (Rosovsky, 1990). For some this is the joy of academic life as it can give one the feeling that her opinions count—or at least must be heard. For others it is living the life of the living-dead. And yet traditional forums like committee meetings, PTA gatherings, and grassroots groups can help generate new ideas (Goodman, 1964). We should not presume that a call for a meeting is tantamount to putting something on hold or sending it to spin aimlessly in a familiar whirlpool of everyone's long-cherished and tightly-clutched opinions. At times we need to look beyond our usual purview to recall what we deem most vital to our teaching.

In line with Bakunin's aphorism (on the epigraph page) concerning the power to think and the desire to rebel, I would encourage you to resist accepting patently any of the answers that this study proposes or the truths that it uncovers. For each chapter in **EDUCATION &** (A)*narchy* is designed to set in motion different ways of thinking about teaching and learning. Specifically, Chapter 1 presents an array of techniques for finding one's way around in the world of literature (though a good case can be made as well for allowing yourself to get lost in a good book), especially as pertains to literary understandings of ethical concerns. Chapter 2 offers a novel approach to arranging and making sense of traditional and historical processes of thought. Chapter 3 attends to the aesthetic component implicit in teaching, and identifies the issues it raises for the assessment of learning. Chapter 4 makes available a series of cases promoting the ethical dimension in continuing education. And Chapter 5 uses athletics in general, and fencing in particular, to show "in other words" what understandably often gets overlooked about the roles we find ourselves taking on in the everyday activities of teaching and learning.

What unites each of these diversely oriented chapters though is that they all provide questions, materials, and sample itineraries that you can adapt and use to think about, and perhaps to rethink, your teaching and learning. The cases and guidelines discussed, however, are not designed to keep you securely ensconced in your "comfort zone." For in much the same way that our students tend to favor one mode of engagement with the material over others and keep coming back to it, we too seek some safe spot where teaching works for us. Once this place has been found, we tend to remain there. To put it colloquially and literally at the same time: we have arrived. But this implies being at the end of a journey and no longer needing to search for, or take to heart, new itineraries of learning. We often work so hard to discover that place of comfort that, even though we may venture out from it at times tentatively if skeptically, we rarely stray too far afield. The errantry of an old-world knight or pilgrim erroneously carries with it today connotations of aimlessness or error, rather than the sense of being on an errand where important messages are delivered and new things are brought back home.

This latter point is pursued as a theme in Chapter 1, so as to set the scene for rediscovering the virtues of just such a course of action. Chapter 2, then, considers the extent to which one's comfort zone is institutionally determined. In real terms, this might take the form of a quiet and orderly classroom or a busy and boisterous one depending on, among other things, your special talents and interests as they stack up to your supervisor's style of administration, and as it stacks up to orders handed down from above, whether a state testing agency, local school board, dean, or special funding source. It might take the form of high marks on student ratings or peer reviews. Whatever form it takes though, such a product-oriented response to the issue of accountability often ends up taking control of our teaching before we have had a chance to reflect on how we might go about letting learning happen. Chapter 3 seeks to make a timely intervention in this seemingly closed circuit by modeling a way of rethinking our place as teachers through a series of incisive, if rudimentary, questions about what teaching is—and what it might be.

For any teacher at any given moment the answer might involve many different, at times contradictory, responses. Often though, it must be allowed, teachers view what they do as a kind of mission; for some it is to inculcate values of one sort or another; for some, to socialize their students; for others it is just to keep the students from hurting themselves, others, or school property. Some teachers see their task as "downloading" information from their field of expertise, the content being determined by perhaps departmental requirements, perhaps state guidelines, or simply one's own level of competence or personal standard of excellence. Some have the goal of getting what is in their head into the heads of their current "crop of students," and end up being extremely frustrated that this is not so easily accomplished. Other teachers with whom I have worked see their job ultimately as being a record keeper in a market-driven credentialing system that answers to ever-larger organizations. Some teachers envision their work as involving grander, less easy to define, missions like opening students' eyes to the beauty of poetry, to the justness of social action, or to the types of discrimination they are likely to encounter in the world (Bushnell, 1996).

Continuing along this line of inquiry, Chapter 4 and Chapter 5 implicitly take into account that, whatever job description, array of tasks, or mission a teacher sees as defining his or her role as an educator, one thread runs through them all: Teachers are the ones who can turn a form of chaos into a kind of order. Sometimes this truth of teaching is cast in stark and ominous terms: "Every teacher's nightmare is losing control of the class" (Schneider, 1998: A12). Until a teacher becomes aware of the extent to which this sense of dread informs his approach to education, you can bet that his day-to-day decisions in the classroom will remain fundamentally reactive in nature. For example, if you have had a problem in the past with late papers upsetting your grading schedule or sense of decorum, then you might implement a policy of giving the offending students penalty grades, lower than what otherwise would have been earned. Or, you might simply refuse to accept late work at all. It goes without saying that the language of economics and mercantile exchange has come to condition, constrain, and guide our thinking about grading (Milton et al., 1986).

Underlying this view is an assumption of dread, one that can haunt one's teaching from the outset. How to keep things from getting out of hand? How to stave off anarchy? It is this aspect of fear, more so than the resulting loss of control, which most poignantly pierces our proverbial body-armor. Fear is one of the three heads of the new Cerberus standing not at the gates of Hades but the Doors of Perception that open onto a rough-hewn path leading to the Creative Imagination [FIGURE 0.1]. The other two heads of this grim canine stopping us in our tracks and thus keeping us from realizing our full potential as teachers and learners are Stress and Habit (Selman et al., 1998).

**FIGURE 0.1**

STRESS

FEAR          HABIT

The New Cerberus

As teachers we worry about a host of tangentially related tasks: implementing curriculum, preparing lesson plans, keeping office hours, caring about our students without intruding too far into their personal lives, fielding unexpected questions in class, assessing students' work "in a timely manner," preparing for outside evaluators, and on and on. Add to this, the stress of administrative surveillance or departmental constraints, peer reviews and other evaluative instruments used for who knows what purpose to accomplish who really knows what end. And nowadays, as any newspaper will tell you, there is a resurgence of the political demagoguery of no-frills basic education on the one hand, and mandated cultural inclusiveness on the other. But even more simply still, you may be afraid that students are too ill-equipped to get all the material you are expected to present, or think they need to know. Whatever pressures lead to your fearfulness though, the end effect is that the educator becomes the one whose role it is to dispel chaos—whether a chaos of partial apprehension on the part of your students, or, what is perhaps worse still, a chaos of half-truths and uninformed opinions kept in circulation by unreflective thinking from either side of the desk.

The teacher, like the administrator (and often the roles overlap), is responsible for quelling chaos. It becomes her responsibility to set in place and to oversee, and to see through to the end, a sense of order. The fear of losing control when engaged in teaching can stifle creative chaos and lead to what might be called fatal order. This book, then, is about recognizing anarchy, and even at times welcoming it, so as to put it to effective use. For when we try to suppress or ignore anarchy—whether within ourselves, our students, or the material we teach—we tend to come down on it so forcefully that invariably it resurfaces elsewhere, and it does so with a vengeance.

Often in the day-to-day dealings in school, as in society at large (of which schools tend to be a kind of carnival mirror image), terms like generalize and imagine are belittled, and the "impressionistic" goals of making connections across disciplines and of "constructing learning" are seen as unnecessary and extra work. Alternatively, terms like "analytical" and "logical" are esteemed highly, and tasks involving "linear processes," like solving math problems or summing up the plot of a story, are seen favorably (perhaps because the results are easy to scan, assess, and grade). Both approaches, of course, are important to the over all goals of teaching and learning, for you can hardly engage meaningfully in generalizations without first using skills of close reading. It is worth keeping in mind that Chapter 1 and Chapter 2 address this situation directly (namely, the importance of developing skills that allow students to read closely for details and critically for broader evaluations); Chapter 3 offers a counter-argument; Chapter 4 puts a different spin on it altogether; and, Chapter 5 cuts across it to find another way into and out of the dilemma it assumes.

The division between the two approaches, between constructivist and traditional models of instruction described above, perhaps is not as pronounced in real life as I have just presented it. Still, I am afraid (and it is a fear borne out by experience) that such polarization haunts academic life. Rather than shy away from this fear, I have taken it on as a main and recurring concern; and, what is more, this book looks at and uses both approaches so as to show how each can inform the other and also point out certain shortcomings. And yet in my choice not to choose one over the other I am likely to draw criticism from people who favor one over the other. This is a risk I am willing to take though because I believe my suggestions can help make a difference in your teaching and learning. I realize that for my ideas to be read and considered, to be taken to heart and implemented, to some extent I needed to write in the familiar discourse of solid argumentation and thereby convince you that these ideas hold water, are air-tight, and ring true.

Anticipating my argument in Chapter 3, I would ask you to pause a moment and listen to what is carried within the very terms we use to speak of clenching an argument. The familiar idioms used to indicate the relative validity of any argument disclose that what is being valued is the sense of completion, wholeness, integrity; what is valued is that which is without breach; chaos averted. Even though I recognize the need to fit my ideas into a form that may, on the surface, seem to dampen the spirit of freedom in which they partake and which they seek to keep alive, I remain confident that something of their wide-ranging applicability will come through.

The power to think and the desire to rebel: Often one's teaching seems to stress one over the other, or actively to suppress one or the other. Sometimes thinking is less important to your goals than just doing what is required; for example, memorizing the material for an examination that you know will be multiple choice, or some other method that tests information retrieval rather than your ability to think creatively and to do something useful with that material. Clever students figure this out early on and are willing to keep in check their desire to rebel (and, in some cases, their desire to learn), except perhaps in small acts of anonymous retaliation, through irreverent behind-the-back impersonations of teachers, peer-group grievance sessions, and other time-honored safety values for letting off steam. The power to think and the desire to rebel: To suppress one is to invite the other to surge up. Yet when one flourishes, so will the other—for neither thinking nor rebelling is to be shunned. Both are natural and yet both are learned. Both thinking and rebelling can occur innocently enough without regard for possible consequences. And yet, at other times, the one feeding off the other, thinking and rebelling can lead to liberation and to sustained reckoning of what has been and charting out where most we need to go next. Standing in opposition to this productive and generative end of thinking and rebelling though is a version of fear that tends to yield a long line of complicit students who are too timid to take risks even in the interest of advancing sincere academic inquiry—students who, when they become teachers, reproduce and often seek to add nothing whatever to the model by which they were trained and tamed (Smith, 1990: 7, 115). It is this variety of fear that we can use to get results from our household pets no less than from our students. It is the variety of spirit-killing fear commented on in the rabbinic *Sifra* on Leviticus 19:3: "What is fear? Not to sit in their seat, or to speak in their place, or to contradict their words."

And yet anarchy dances hand in hand with education if learning is destined to occur. For no matter how much it may be feared or short-circuited, anarchy remains a vital, if unspoken, component—and is perhaps the motivating factor—of lasting learning. Our responses to anarchy may differ, but whatever form it takes you can be sure that it shows up in the various ways our teaching, like our learning and like our administrating, is colored by fear: our fear that things will fall apart, that a program will not work because we have never tried it that way; our fear that we cannot teach (or learn) what or how we want to teach (or learn) because someone over us might not approve; our concern that we might lose our funding unless we can described our study's results more succinctly or use more current citations. . . . Fear and Habit rear their heads and set Stress to barking.

Anarchy does not stand in opposition to order whether in education or in politics. Each is part of the other; and though one may prevail for a spell, the other could appear at any time. Neither is wholly positive nor wholly negative, since, after all, they keep one another in check and in motion—constant motion. To put it philosophically, they exist in a dialectical relation to one another, but only insofar as that is how they have been conceptualized traditionally in Western thinking. The Taoist principle of Yin/Yang offers a useful corrective, though I am quick to add that we cannot, with the wave a hand, banish from our thinking long-standing cultural biases or commonplaces. It takes time before new metaphors (or old ones from the East) can be played out meaningfully and come to rest authentically in the theatres of our minds. Universally, though, there seems to be a special delight we take in putting things in their place, just as there is in creating new places and novel ways of putting things there. And, as language-users, we have learned to speak, and perhaps even to think, in strings and clusters and meaningful patterns—a point taken for granted in Chapter 1 and turned inside-out in Chapter 3.

The same holds for finding one's place in the world and social relations, and this is especially true in schools. For example students, like anyone attuned to the ways that others exercise power over them and seek to maintain control over them and their peer group, respond well to consistent guidelines. We all like to know where we stand and what is expected of us. What we do from here though is a matter of conviction. Aislinn Vaughan helped me recognize what is easy to lose sight of amidst all that a teacher is called on to do beyond classroom instruction. She remarked that when there is a choice, irrespective of the subject matter, a student will sign up to take courses from a teacher who she believes (whether from first-hand experience or hear-say) will respect her, care about her intellectual and academic needs at least, and who will take her ideas seriously. She commented further how important she thought it was that a teacher would go "to the trouble of carefully explaining his goals for the class (and typing them up rather than just voicing them), his expectations, and what he hopes the students would gain from his lectures and from the selected texts" (Vaughan, 1998).

Of course this desire to know what outcomes one is expected to perform can be taken to extremes, as in the immemorial "Will that be on the exam?" But we should not be aggravated with students over this, for aren't we—as upholders of the institutional guidelines and standards, whether by default or in earnest—responsible for teaching them this along with whatever else we sought to impart regarding course content? Some teachers build "choice" into the structure of the test: "Answer any three of the following five questions." But this is just the flip side of a student's anxious question about what to expect on Judgment Day. Do not be deceived into thinking that such alternatives, still squarely within the framework of the conventional mold, ever can take you far beyond the hollow concession of substituting one book for another, of giving similar but slightly different problem sets, of assigning a take-home exam instead of the equally (or more stressful) final examination.

Such substitutions are cosmetic and do not get at the deeper issue: namely, that there is something counter-productive to learning when teachers rely exclusively on expedient ways of testing and assessing what is supposed to have been learned. To be sure, with all of the pressures and time-constraints put on teachers who often have to "process" more students than is reasonable to expect of them, it is little wonder that some faculty members roll their eyes when changes in their routines are mentioned or mandated. Habit rears its heavy head and bumps up against Stress and Fear—the stress of even more work on top of what one already has and the fear that you will not meet your timetable or quotas of whatever kind. Wherever each of us comes down on this issue though, I believe that: Just as we should not be vague or inconsistent when revealing guidelines and deadlines, we should be forthcoming and clear both about our grading procedures and how we intend to educate our students. But the issue of grading and assessment has been studiously sidestepped; it is conspicuously off the map of the ground that is covered in this book [FIGURE 0.2].

The material covered though, in Chapter 1, concerns ways that the issue of grading can be absorbed into your creative forays into classroom management and bookkeeping of symbols (by which I mean grades). "Classroom Capers" looks into the history of the topic and then sets the parameters for further inquiry using a five-fingered memory image to express the main points covered (see the first stage, "I.," shown on FIGURE 0.2, though the five discrete memory images on the front of the hand are concealed here, they are revealed on FIGURE 1.13 and analyzed in the middle section of Chapter 1). The cases discussed in this chapter provide a range of handy ways to anticipate, diffuse, and channel the shock that attends anarchy's interplay with order in the classroom. Here the Memory Arts are shown to be an age-old and yet revolutionary way to revive and implement styles of visual and aural learning. Here we explore the impulse in teaching to keep chaos at bay while recognizing that anarchy interacts with order. Anarchy shows up most vividly when we are confronted with limiting the scope of infinity; for example, when devising a course covering a thousand years of literary developments. In "Classroom Capers," as elsewhere, I have interspersed students' illustrations and comments, so as to present a variety of responses to my experiments with and attempts at finding appropriate ways

**FIGURE 0.2**

MAP OF THE BOOK

to help students discover how they can accept more responsibility for their own education. Their drawings and graphic charts completed in the context of literary-based courses, in the end, communicate worlds beyond what their words on the same topic might have revealed. The latter method, however, I would point out, was my original plan for the book. When I began this project I wanted to minimize the presence of my own voice and let students speak triumphantly for themselves and about what they had learned about learning. Through trial and error though, I learned—and had to admit—that the words of others, even when seemingly left to speak for themselves, always end up reflecting their status as having been carefully arranged by someone else. The more I sought to erase my presence, the more it intruded on the form of the book.

Notwithstanding this change in how I am presenting the content of **EDUCATION &** (A)*narchy*, I remain committed to learning how to listen more carefully to what students have to say because, all too often, we only get to hear exactly what we have asked them to say. And so, here again, grading shows itself to be the proverbial tail wagging the educational dog. It is hardly surprising then that "grade inflation" is a hot-button topic trotted out at opportune times in institutions of higher learning. Evoking the dark specter of inflation overshadows any discussion about more pertinent and far-reaching topics, like the social implications of such marks among various peer groups; like the very real economic consequences such marks have for the students down the road, whether for good or ill; like the ethical consequences involved in the changing of grades for whatever the extracurricular end prompting it, which in itself points out the often arbitrary nature of how they are assigned in the first place. When grade inflation is discussed, most people straighten up and look serious and concerned for there is an overriding fear that the values represented by these symbols are deviating from . . . well, from what? Are the teachers grading too lightly or are they making the tests too easy? Grades are, in fact, symbols that tend to conceal the nature and quality of the tests through which they were derived (Dressel, 1983). We can endow grades with as much power over us, and over our teaching, as we choose. In this grading is like a Frankenstein-monster, made in our own worst image, a monster that will continue to dog us until we stop and confront it in the icy wasteland, and try to understand this pitiful, this mechanical and dreadful, reflection of our culture and of ourselves (see again FIGURE 0.2, drifting to the left of the map showing the ground covered).

Hence my "call to thinking" in Chapter 2, supplemented with a tidy chart used to organize the main ways questioning is realized (II. on FIGURE 0.2 [referring to FIGURE 2.2]); and, in Chapter 3, my focus on how products tend to be valued in the process of assessing learning outcomes (see III. on FIGURE 0.2, the crossed paint-brush and pencil, emblems of the visual and verbal arts, hovering in the air between sea and land). The central chapter of the book though, "Speaking of Teaching," shines a steady and concentrated beam of light on the stolid relationship which, over time, has come to characterize the interplay of product and process. The chapter thus is an extended meditation on what exactly is being done when we speak of making art, a meditation intended to be applied to other disciplines and areas of study across the board.

Following from this, Chapter 4 raises questions that hinge on a critical distinction between education and schooling. Education can happen any time, at any place—even in school; while schooling is bound to specific places and times, to specific windows opened for learning and then closed when the bell rings (hence the luminous book represented at Stage IV. on FIGURE 0.2). The end of schooling is a credential; the end of education, however is. . . . **EDUCATION &** *(A)narchy* grapples with how that sentence might be finished, by keeping in play two seemingly opposed attitudes toward education. On the one hand, we have the "Pedagogy of Permission and Self Reliance" ("follow in earnest your interests and findings where they lead you"); and, on the other, the more pragmatic "Pedagogy of Punishment and Consequences" ("do this by then, or else"). The Pedagogy of Permission implies an approach to learning that has little to do with dread; it is an approach which bolsters one's desire to succeed and which diminishes one's fear of failing. As this chapter admits, it is hard to judge how much really is learned when someone is compelled to take classes, whether for credit or to keep a license current. Under the heading of "required for major" and "continuing education," a lot of schooling is going on. How then to transform it, realizing that any attempt at transformation always has consequences? In the tussle and tug of these two approaches in striving to overcome one another, even though we may be partial to one over the other, they each propel the other farther than either could take us on its own. This is part of the recurring cycle in anarchy's immemorial gyration with order; this is the turning, the revolution, that lets learning happen.

Chapter 5 tackles head-on the day-to-day capering of permission and punishment, of anarchy and order, and uses an analogy to argue that it is acceptable, even laudable (and perhaps necessary for the well-being of the spirit of education), to try out forms of instruction that are different from those with which you are most familiar. It is not easy though to think beyond or outside of the organizing principles that currently hold our classes, schools, and funding foundations in place. With this in mind, "The Sword of Truth" concludes by inquiring when and to what extent we have a voice in how we define ourselves as teachers, no less than as learners (hence, the fifth and final stage shown on FIGURE 0.2, swirling into a vortex, the crossed swords pointing to and overseen by the Hebrew root word למד [LMD], out of which teaching and learning both are formed). But before we can come up with a provisional answer to this inquiry though, we need to take into account our own educational background and biases, our preferred teaching style and learning habits, and what we value about the life of learning. Also we need to consider how we came to be teachers in the first place. In my own case, it would be disingenuous for me to abandon or overlook what might be termed traditional pedagogy. For how can we even begin to conceptualize what we do as teachers without recourse to the tradition within which we have been trained? In my assumption of the tradition, and in my insistence on the judicious use of repetition, I would quote the following (and will do so again in Chapter 3).

> The assumption of the tradition is *not* necessarily traditionalism and the adoption of prejudices. The *genuine repetition* of a traditional ques-tion lets its external character as a tradition fade away and pulls back from the prejudices. . . . Thus, the contact with the tradition, the return to history, can have a double sense. On the one hand, it can be purely a matter of traditionalism, in which what is assumed is itself not subjected to criticism. On the other hand, however, the return can also be performed so that it goes back *prior* to the questions which were posed in history, and the questions raised by the past are once again originally appropriated (Heidegger, 1992: 138).

Like Arnold (who is quoted on the epigraph page), I realize that this is all part of the real-life negotiating that goes on every day in so many ways. And so in the face of what might at first glance appear to be contradictions in my relation to the tradition and to traditionalism where pedagogical practices are concerned, I have sought to acknowledge them and to take them in stride rather than ignore them or pretend that they somehow do not affect how I tend to teach and to learn. Indeed, while Chapter 1 draws on my years of teaching in university settings, the ensu-ing four chapters are a result of my changing teaching venues and having to improvise accordingly. Chapter 2 takes the first preliminary step away from college-level instruction toward teaching high-school teachers and department heads drawing on the mnemonic practices disclosed in Chap-ter 1. Stepping out a little further from what for years I had come to consider my teaching "comfort zone," Chapter 3 is a reflection of my experiences working with school administrators and with grade-school students in areas where letter grades are not assigned—areas like art. Chapter 4, which moves deeper into the world of continuing education programs, concerns my teaching and research in ethics and the canons of law. And Chapter 5 comes out of my experiences as a fencer, and more recently as a person who has been trained and certified to teach the sport as well. Since leaving the university, the world has become my classroom.

Throughout **EDUCATION &** *Anarchy* I have tried to strike a series of balances, mainly between theoretical speculation and practical considerations; between recursive questioning to get at the bottom of things and common sense to keep what is obvious in plain view. I have tried to take into account both the kind of teaching that goes on in schools, and also that which takes place outside the usual institutional structure. I have maintained a balance between plans of action conceived in the past and also those unique to our own time. In striking these balances I have sought, above all else, to present a range of creative possibilities and decisive options that can be easily adapted to suit your current needs, and in so doing to give you an occasion to reflect on how you will go about putting your students first. "We cannot organize you. It will depend upon *you* what sort of organization you will choose" (Kropotkin, 1886-1907/1988: 32).

# Chapter 1

## Classroom Capers

### I. Grounding

Once in Pasadena, at the Crocodile Café, I marveled that our server got all of our orders exactly right without writing anything down. I asked her how she did it. She said she went around the table and imagined each of our meals placed in front of us. Little did she know that she was echoing the method of Simonides, founder of the ancient Art of Memory.

The story goes that one night, at a grand banquet, the ceiling collapsed killing everyone inside. The bodies were so mangled that the mourners could not identify the remains of their relatives until Simonides, who earlier that evening had sung a hymn in praise of "The Twins," Castor and Pollux, happened to remember where each person had been sitting. Tradition has it that Simonides was called away just prior to the catastrophe by two mysterious strangers who vanished once he was safely outside (Yates, 1978).

I have a friend, Richard Johnson, who, like Simonides, is a musician. He has brought the house down many a time, but only metaphorically. He has hundreds of songs in his repertoire—most without words. How does he remember them, let alone keep them straight in his mind? He told me once that when he composes or learns a new song, he plays the first line then that one plus the next and so on, adding a new line each time until he has gotten the whole piece by heart. But, he added, the only way really to get it down is by playing it in its entirety over and over again. That way each section opens onto the next in succession, each part being integral to the coherence of the whole.

The server and the guitarist just mentioned each have found patterns that help them recall what they need to know to carry out their work in the world. I have long been intrigued with the seemingly natural ways we come up with artificial means to enhance and activate our memories. The classroom has been ideal place for me to learn more about the Memory Arts, and, over the years, I have developed an approach to teaching that enables students to experiment with, and thus discover and take to heart, resplendent shades of meaning in what they study. Mainly this is facilitated through worksheets and study guides collectively known as "capers." I am indebted to R.J. Stegner, my high school English teacher and debate coach, for this snappy and apt term and for inducting me into the mysteries of capering. Capers are spirited leaps of thought. They are lively dances for the mind that can be done alone or in groups, whether in class or on one's own time.

David Rushton found capers to be the life-blood of my own teaching. And he should know since he had the distinction, among other things, of being the first and only student while I was teaching at Vanderbilt to take two freshman seminars. Students received credit for only one freshman seminar, so why sign up for a second after the requirement had been fulfilled? But David wanted to pursue some issues raised by his Fall seminar. In an unprecedented move, he petitioned the Dean to let him enroll in a second freshman seminar, one which I happened to be scheduled to teach that Spring. It is to David's credit that he was undaunted by the several sets of forms-in-triplicate he had to fill out and return within 48 hours—the kinds of regulations and paper-barriers that tend to deter most undergraduates (or graduate students for that matter) from attempting anything out of the ordinary. In an essay examining what and how he had learned during the course, David wrote:

> Capers captured the essence of Engel's teaching. Each class meeting embodied a caper in its spontaneity, energy, and flexibility. Yet, specifically labeled "caper days" evoke memories of class exercises guided by handouts or other preconceived plans. These outlines did not hinder the exploration by any means. Each caper achieved Engel's goal—to proffer a new lens for reflection—because his familiarity with the caper's trajectory enabled him to coax discussion and thought toward key ideas. The ideas abruptly unmasked preconceptions. In Nietzschean termi-

nology, they provoke unlearning, or the revaluation of values. For example, Engel's forcing the class to cheat on a mock-quiz, including a pledged statement of cheating instead of honor, laid bare the significance of honesty. Once grasped these key ideas opened an array of doors—potential individual capers for the student (Rushton, 1998).

Sometimes the same caper can be assigned at different times during the term so students can see and reflect on just how far they have come along in their thinking about the larger thematic concerns. For example, on one caper that was given at the beginning of term and again at the end, which was described as being a "Personalized Epistemeter: A way to think about what you think you know during Spring Term, 1996," David remarked: "The first handout being printed on white, the second green. The second one was brand new to me" [FIGURE 1.1]. Such an inventory helps students take stock of what constitutes their point of view; it helps them decide from where they are starting and thus enables them to determine what changes, if any, have taken place in their thinking over the course of the term. It is my policy not to evaluate or make judgments about the students' work based on such subjective capers, but to let it serve them as personal heuristic instruments.

Capers involving more traditional forms of knowledge, for example on the construction of a sonnet, can be assigned at different intervals in the term as well. The rationale is simple: students are likely to approach a caper differently and more experimentally the second time around. After all they have already seen what doing it one particular way looks like and they know what sorts of results they can expect. This form of repetition need not be redundant though because there is always something else to be said about the topic and alternative ways of expressing it.

Capers are not simply study-guides or convenient ways for teachers to assess the extent to which students are keeping up with assignments, though to be sure they fulfill both of these functions. More than this, capers are like windows to the soul of the curriculum. As a result they make it possible for students to project where they want to go once they have seen the larger picture by virtue of having pieced together the component parts in ways that make sense to them.

Through a series of controlled and on-going experiments with curriculum, I have found that retrieving and modifying some of the more lucid of the ancient memory schemes, like the one advocated by Simonides, enables students to produce work that goes far beyond what

**Figure 1.1**

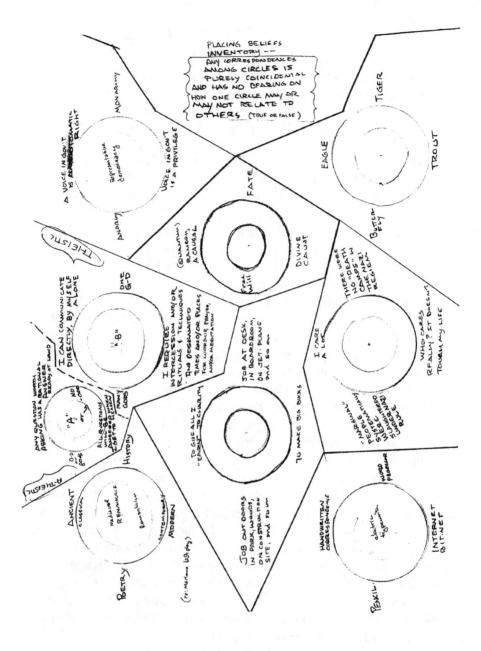

one might otherwise expect of them. The judicious use of artificial memory schemes, or mnemonics as they are more commonly called, not only strengthens natural memory (to reiterate an age-old claim among proponents of the Memory Arts) and leads to greater comprehension of material, but also—and which is more laudable still—gives one the means and inclination to apply in the world the ethical lessons one has encountered in books.

Mnemonics can be generative and dynamic learning tools. They need not be viewed as convoluted, contrived ways to conjure what you want to recall. They need not be treated as tricks for locating, and short cuts for retrieving, previously buried information. To be sure though, students in most traditional classrooms are called upon to dig up that information; they need to know where the proverbial bone was placed and how to get at it as quickly as possible. But once these tasks are accomplished and the bone brought back, what will be done with it? Will Fido simply show it to the master so it can be tossed out once more and the game of fetch continue until grades are assigned? Gnawing on it further only will reduce it to nothing—and nothing will have been gained beyond the exercise. Often this is the case when students are made to learn isolated facts by rote. Only when many such bones are retrieved, and along with them the treasures that are unearthed in the process, can something more exciting and vital take place. When these dry bones have been recollected, arranged, and recovered; when they have been animated by the wind and spirit of the Art of Memory; then we are in a position to build anew the body of knowledge which, to echo Ezekiel's allegorical vision, shall rise and live again.

Insofar as the innovation in education I am proposing here is based on ancient principles, it is, in the true sense of the term, revolutionary. The root word means to turn back or to turn over, hence the more radical implication of over-turning a dominant, or persistent, paradigm, whether in science, political life, or education. It is high time that we turned back to, and recycled, views on education pertaining to the Memory Arts, a philosophy of learning which takes into account and which respects differences among students' needs and abilities. In so doing, we will find that mnemonics are truly constructive—and can serve us well in building anew the Palace of Wisdom.

\* \* \* \* \*

The history of the Memory Arts is long and venerable. In what amounts to bookkeeping tablets of ancient Sumeria we have cuneiform evidence of mnemonic groupings used to record the storage and distribution of vast amounts of grain, wine, and other commodities. Once the Arts of Memory were institutionalized, though, they were used primarily in connection with oratory, law, commerce, and the perennial activity of networking. For example, Alexander the Great inspired intense loyalty among his men during his periodic troop-reviews: he called them by name, congratulated them on their specific feats of valor in battles recent and old, and knew who to ask about a wife and who about a child—and this from a man who assembled the largest army in the ancient world. Of course he did have Aristotle for a teacher, that remarkable biologist who systematized all branches of knowledge, and whose logical method held sway well into the European Enlightenment and which, even in modern times, has enjoyed something of a revival (Crane, 1967).

Even before Aristotle though, memory, as the cornerstone of Plato's theory of knowledge, prepared the foundation for philosophy and psychology in the West. As a result, handbooks on the practical applications of mnemonics go back at least to the first century. Using these techniques Seneca, the great Stoic philosopher, is said to have been able to hear a list of a hundred random items only once and then could repeat it, whether backward or forward. Despite such amazing feats of mental gymnastics though, from the very beginning it is clear that the Memory Arts were associated with the most profound topics no less than the most mundane affairs of the world.

Rhetorical training texts from Cicero to Descartes regularly included schemes and methods for condensing the things you wanted to remember into symbols or images, which then were to be placed, in sequence, around a table, room, theatre, mansion, or city, so eventually they can be retrieved, reconstituted, and applied as the occasion demanded (Yates, 1978). Survivals of this technique still mark our language. For example, when going through a list of reasons we say: "in the first place" and "passing on to the next point." The handbooks sought to reinforce one's capacity readily and creatively to visualize things. The same holds true today regarding "organizational" and "encoded mnemonics" (Bellezza, 1987). Before background images ("organizational mnemonics") can be brought into play though, the student needs to come up with useful and distinct trigger symbols and letter cues ("encoded mnemonics").

For example, with regard to the latter case, a popular short-cut to learning, usually referred to simply as a mnemonic device, might involve taking the first letter of the words you want to recall and visualizing them arranged perhaps on your hand or a page in a book. For example, GELND can be used to recall the first five books of the Bible (**G**enesis, **E**xodus, **L**eviticus, **N**umbers, and **D**euteronomy). And yet, insofar as this letter-string does not spell a recognizable word, it may be harder to remember than something that does have an identifiable and more readily accessible point of connection. And so, closely related to this technique, is the creation of a mnemonic sentence formed from a string of words in which the first letter of each word corresponds to one in the target sequence. For example, to recall the twelve signs of the zodiac, you might take the first letter, or even the first syllable of each (**A**ries, **T**aurus, **Gem**ini, **C**ancer, **L**eo) and if possible making use of semantic associations ("**Virtuous**" for **Vir**go the **Vir**gin) and so on (**Li**bra, **S**corpio, **S**agittarius, **Capric**orn, **A**quarius, **P**isces) to come up with: **Ariel Taught: Gems Can Let Virtuous Light Scatter So Capric**iously **A . . . s Prisms**.

Such a device, for some, may be more difficult to use than simply committing the twelve signs to memory, perhaps by visualizing the designated animals and figures as being superimposed onto the constellations, star by star—like connecting the dots—and then visualize them dancing around a heavenly belt or clock's face. But even so, once such a visual scheme is memorized, of what practical use is it? How is this more than a rote memory trick? How does this knowledge transfer? I believe it is more than mere trickery, and that the knowledge thus derived and stored does transfer readily and easily into other areas and disciplines. This chapter will argue, in fact, that this is the case, both with respect to the Art of Memory understood as a method for generating, collecting, and analyzing useful information, as well as with respect to showing us ways of living more reflective and virtuous lives. In what follows I want to clarify the various ends that such a practice, as both method and practical plan, can be said to prefigure.

Often we can lose our way, whether when reciting a poem or along the road of life itself. All it takes is for someone to intervene and give us the beginning of a line or help us recall where we left off, and then the rest will come flooding back to us. Once we have recovered our place, or perhaps found it for the first time, then we can proceed on our way. It is always a relief and personal triumph to recover what we feared had "slipped our mind." And so, both regarding poetry and life, such place-holders need not be static; they can be dynamic and generative.

For example, memory techniques for recitation go hand in hand with the composition of epic poetry, like Homer's *Iliad* and *Odyssey*. The same is true for Anglo-Saxon sagas, which were meant to be recited and heard aloud. Poems like *Beowulf,* with its intricate and interlocking ring-structure, brought sound and meaning together through sonorous devices like alliteration and semantic couplings known as kennings. The lays of wandering troubadours during the middle ages were indebted to the full panoply of rhetorical and mnemonic devices. Indeed, in a world where few could read or write, a good memory was essential. It was for this reason that rhyme, a useful *aide-memoire*, was the prevalent form of popular literature in the Gothic period. Up to the fourteenth century almost all secular texts, except legal documents, were written in rhyme. Medieval French merchants used a poem made up of 137 rhyming couplets, which contained all rules of commercial arithmetic (Burke, 1985: 99). On a purely academic level then, we can see how rudimentary knowledge of mnemonic techniques gives us insight into how works of literature were composed—or, at least, were organized. For example recent and sustained work on Montaigne's *Essais* reveals that the great essayist had in mind a three-tiered architectural model for organizing and displaying his 107 essays (Martin, 1996). But beyond the sheer achievement of the textual archeology involved in recovering such a hidden design—whether or not we are convinced that Montaigne had this exact model in mind when he penned his essays—such a scheme has the added benefit of giving the modern reader access to a monument of the Western literary tradition.

The history of mnemonics is long and mostly venerable. Notwithstanding intellectual giants like Bruno and Descartes who used mnemonics to advance the frontiers of human knowledge, there have always been hucksters and entrepreneurs promising amazing results if you buy into their particular memory system. Still familiarity with the tradition helps to focus on what kinds of cues and techniques will make for the best capers in a given venue, situation, or classroom context. Basically though the ancient rhetorical tracts, like contemporary self-help books advertising easy ways to improve your memory, reiterate what commonsense tells us: long-term retention is based on fixing something in mind, perhaps through an associative link, and then the connection is stabilized and strengthened through repetition. Further, I would have us keep ever in mind two closely related questions that are fundamental to successful classroom capering: Once something has been targeted to be retained, with respect to what is it lodged? And to what end? The rest of this section responds to these questions by outlining the theory underlying effective capers.

Consider for example that from the vast storehouse of recorded precedents a judge discriminates and selects those that enable her to construct a coherent legal decision; so too the epic-poet relies on a vast magazine of rhetorical conventions and tropological traditions to craft an enduring and original poem. In both cases the internal logic underlying the finished product can be retraced and easily followed once you have identified—and placed—these main points into some sort of organizational plan.

This enables the salient and constituent parts to come into focus and thus to be retrieved in sequence. Sometimes you can use the original as a kind of skeletal structure allowing you later to "flesh out" the "bare bones" of the argument as it is written. For example, John Milton, at the recommendation of his friend Andrew Marvell, added a narrative "Argument" of the main events covered in each book of *Paradise Lost* so that his future readers would not find themselves, like the fallen demons in Book Two, "in wand'ring mazes lost." Other times you can invent mnemonic markers to chart a course that may enable you to do more than simply recall the gist of the argument [FIGURE 1.2] (Crump, 1975).

One of the main advantages of this type of approach is that you are more likely to notice things in the original that otherwise would have remained undetected. For example, if you are mapping out the argument of Plato's *Republic* and neglect to attend to the trajectory of allegorical comparisons, then you might miss seeing how Socrates' analogies parallel the unfolding of the dialogue's main theme concerning the quest to define justice. (This will be taken up at greater length in Chapter 4, in the context of teaching Plato to adults in a "not for credit" seminar.)

Sometimes we need to chart the movements of a work on its own terms if we hope to recover the special epistemology informing its aesthetic character. For example, the sentence-structure of William Faulkner's *Light in August* provides clues about how people reflect on their experiences, which in turn characterizes how they come to know, even if they refuse to accept, their place in the world. While the events depicted in this novel can be reconstructed and put in a chronology (and this is useful so long as you do not stop there), any effort to impose such

## Figure 1.2

Chiastic Plan
of the 12 Book Structure of Milton's *Paradise Lost* (1674 – 2<sup>nd</sup> edition)

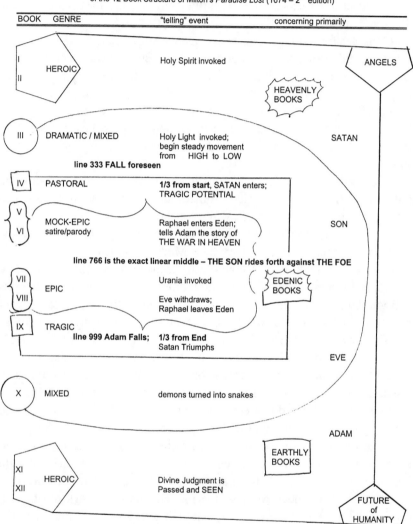

a linear template onto the narrative design would be misguided and ultimately irresponsible. Consider for example the lines opening chapter six, lines which resonate purposefully with this chapter's main theme as well:

Memory believes before knowing remembers. Believes longer than recollects, longer than knowing even wonders. Knows remembers believes a corridor in a big long garbled cold echoing building of dark red brick sootbleakened by more chimneys than its own, set in a grassless cinderstrewnpacked compound surrounded by smoking factory purlieus and enclosed by a ten foot steel-and-wire fence like a penitentiary or a zoo, where in random erratic surges . . . (Faulkner, 1932/1972: 111).

Faulkner's prose conveys—even as it models—the way that memory sets things in motion; how once it is cued to bring back the scattered image, it grabs as it goes and is off and running. It pulls back the past by relocating a residual pattern that needs only to be filled in and colored once more as it used to be. And now it can be recognized, and, at last, known again. And yet it is known in a new way both because of the gathering process and also because of where the knower now is situated. This is the key to understanding the recollective narrative design of Faulkner's novel. It is also an example of how anarchy is, in part, organized through the regime of words. Yet even words are part of that chaos of the past that floods into one's carefully marked off present, which unfiltered renders the raw truths of one's existence. The order of language both brings coherence to it and yet makes its truths subject to the undifferentiated chaos of half-remembered experience. We sense there is something to be retrieved, and in turning back. . . . "Memory believes before knowing remembers."

When using mnemonic designs of whatever sort to set in play this kind of recollective design, what matters above all else is the relative ease with which you can regain your points of access and your cues for retrieving those points. Only then can you build on it and do something with it that moves beyond mere recollection so as to see how it might be a bridge to other areas of endeavor. For example, students can begin to make sense of the sweep of literary history from, say, *Beowulf* to *Paradise Lost* by reading "manageable chunks" of representative works while allowing themselves to be guided by capers that focus their attention on points of contrast and comparison, contiguity and tangency [FIGURE 1.3]. For example even when focusing on just fifty lines of *Beowulf* one student, Harriet Goodrich, noticed how the epithet "solitary fiend"— referring to Grendel, the first monster Beowulf battles—was set off against the terms used to describe the community of noble warriors and the friendship-banquet. Likewise, the words used to describe the darkness

# Figure 1.3

FITT # **II** ; pages 55-59 NAME: M ☺ HARRIET GOODRICH
USE PEN OR PRINT DARKLY AS THIS SHEET WILL BE XEROXED FOR CAPERS

1. **ON THE BACK**, chart out the genealogies of the MAIN CHARACTERS, and be sure to indicate various alliances, affinities, and "directions of affect."
2. **ON THE BACK**, chart out (whether graphically and/or in ciphers and/or in memory images) the key points in the Fitt's action so as to reconstruct the main movements in action and poetry.

3. Articulate succinctly what happens in your Fitt. Tell what is going on. This is the narrative counterpart to your diagrams on the back.

After the Danes are asleep following their banquet, Grendel comes and takes thirty men from the hall for his own feast. Hrothgar, very attached to his people, grieves. Grendel's attacks and Hrothgar's grieving continue for "twelve winters." ✓ The council men during this period attempt to find a plan to go against Grendel; ~~and~~ they ar are unsuccessful. The fitt ends with a contrast between negative and positive: the unfortunate do not know God, while those who do may seek his protection.

4. Give several notable kennings, epithets, uses of litotes, and so on:
• "unholy spirit" - Grendel - also, "monstrous enemy", "devilish spirit", "death-shadow", "solitary fiend"
• "King-Danes" - thanes; bound to line 80 - Hrothgar shared his wealth with them
• "Scylding king" - Hrothgar - lineage description
• "jewel-decorated" - Heorot
• "Judge of our deeds", "King of Glory" - God
Litotes: - "they knew no sorrow", "man's sad lot", "- was too deep in sin", "- he knew not His love."

5. List a few Anglo-Saxon terms that seem to carry within them the kernel of modern equivalents. Does anything strike you about these?
Be sure to indicate any key words that RECUR throughout your Fitt.
æfter - after ...
bēor - beer
grim - fierce (meanings)
wæs - war, was
twelf wintra - twelve winters ✓
wið - with

manna - men ⎫
men - men ⎬ the same: man invented language
man - man ⎭
wel - well
dēað - death $\overline{\text{See}}$ FOR FREE: pp. 232-33, ℓ. 3037.   GOOD JOB
niht, nihtum, nihte - recurs for night, follows theme

6. Identify two moments in the Fitt that are the most MEMORABLE for you (not necessarily those "central" to the epic as a whole) and then justify your selection.

p. 57, line 125: The image of a "slaughtered feast of men" reminds me of a prime-time news report about a serial killer. This ~~voca~~ choice of words provokes an undesirable memory. I also find Or the difference in description between the Danes' banquet and the villian Grendel's banquet interesting — the adjectives/word choice match the subjects.

of Grendel's realm as well as his sullen nature was set in sharp contract to the "jewel decorated" mead hall with its brightness and sounds of joy. Harriet also noted a curious and gruesome irony in the description of good-natured carousing at the feast *among* men in the great hall at the heart of the kingdom, known as Heorot, set off aginst Grendel's solitary feast *of* men in the marshy outlands. As her caper indicates (and which, as a result of having completed in advance of the class meeting, she was able to discuss authoritatively) there is a series of words, like darkness, that showed up at key junctures later in the poem (beyond the fifty lines for which she was the designated class expert). Once clued in to look for such *tag words* (something that will be discussed at greater length in the next section), she could track the various uses of the term as she continued reading and, thereby, was in a position to remark on subtle differences in the shades of its meaning. She remarked that the language functioned like music in a mystery movie sound track. This was an appropriate comparison indeed, one building on her response to #6 regarding the image of a "slaughtered feast of men" which reminded her of a prime-time news report about a serial killer—one who, like Grendel, was motivated by his envy of others' happiness and fellowship which he could never hope to experience. Thus this kind of caper helps students find apt contemporary comparisons to comment on how the same emotions and themes were expressed and conveyed a thousand years ago. Indeed the comparisons made and contrasts observed, like the image patterns discovered, need not be those intended by the author. It is in this respect that contingency and tangency come into play in the contemporary classroom, as they provide vital points of contact with, and connection to, great works of art and literature.

And the same applies when we line up a series of such works seen one with respect to the others by building on the kinds of capers just described, resulting in a memorable *grid* (which will be discussed at greater length in the next section) [FIGURE 1.4]. Such a caper not only helps students condense a great deal of information into easy to recall parcels of raw data, but also can provide subtle insights into the books that otherwise might have remained invisible, connections that would have gone unnoticed. It has the added benefit of allowing students to compare their grids with one another, to discuss and to argue intelligently about differences among their responses. Students are quick to tell one another when someone's information flat-out is wrong, because they quickly realize that a valid interpretation of a textual quibble or a

# Figure 1.4

YOUR PERSONALIZED MEMORY GRID    NAME: _(illegible)_
to record and construct (for easy recall, days or years hence) mnemic-bites) mnemic-bites – _littlesecb_  ( ✓ )
and to use as a model for your graphic SHIELD SURVEY due on Mon 11 Dec 95 of memory

| | Beowulf | CT, Ind (BOU) | SPENSER | Sidney | Sh LLL | Sk. "El" | H&L, WYATT, SURREY |
|---|---|---|---|---|---|---|---|
| subjectively rank by − + | + | + | + | − | + | | + |
| title & dating; author's name | Beowulf / bef. C7th and 8th / unknown | Bk of Duch / 1498 / John Skelton | Faerie Queen I–III / 1590–1596 / Edmund Spenser | Astrophil and Stella / 1582 / Sir Philip Sidney | Love's Labor Lost / 1595 / Wm. Shakespeare | Elegy _(illeg.)_ / 1517 / John Skelton | Hero and Leander / 1593 / Christopher Marlowe |
| genre; kind of work it is; models... | heroic poem _(illegible handwriting)_ | _(illegible handwriting)_ | _(illegible handwriting)_ | _(illegible handwriting)_ | comic, satire play _(illeg.)_ | lyric / poems _(illeg.)_ | lyrical narrative both heroic/romantic and mock-heroic at same time |
| characteristic features of style, tropes | _(illegible handwriting)_ | _(illegible handwriting)_ | _(illegible handwriting)_ | _(illegible handwriting)_ | _(illegible handwriting)_ | iambic _(illeg.)_ | _(illegible handwriting)_ |
| content summed and its place in the sweep of ENGL lit & cult | _(illegible handwriting)_ | _(illegible handwriting)_ | _(illegible handwriting)_ | _(illegible handwriting)_ | _(illegible handwriting)_ | _(illegible handwriting)_ | _(illegible handwriting)_ |
| something else true & accurate | _(illegible handwriting)_ | _(illegible handwriting)_ | _(illegible handwriting)_ | _(illegible handwriting)_ | _(illegible handwriting)_ | _(illegible handwriting)_ | _(illegible handwriting)_ |
| summed up | _(illegible handwriting)_ | _(illegible handwriting)_ | _(illegible handwriting)_ | _(illegible handwriting)_ | _(illegible handwriting)_ | _(illegible handwriting)_ | _(illegible handwriting)_ |

narrative issue depends on its being grounded on the facts. It is for this reason that I regularly include at least one question or category on each caper that asks explicitly for something on the order of "something else true and accurate" [second from the bottom on the left, FIGURE 1.4].

The limits placed on class-sessions and the demands put on students' time in general—the practical exigencies of college-level instruction— impelled me originally to work creatively with course requirements and intellectual expectations. I believed it was unrealistic to expect that students in one semester could read all of the works one might expect traditionally to find on just such a survey course syllabus, let alone make informed aesthetic and cultural determinations about them, namely: *Beowulf*, Chaucer's *Canterbury Tales*, Sidney's *Astrophil and Stella*, Spenser's *Faerie Queene*, a play by Shakespeare and one by Marlowe, Milton's *Paradise Lost*, plus a sampling of less canonical works (for example, recently recovered works by and about women, tracts and journals concerning the slave trade and encounters with the New World). I did not lower my expectations but sought to bring them in line with a different curricular aim. And so, I kept to this modest, bare-bones, syllabus of major figures and came up with a way to get students excited about reading a reasonable amount of each of the assigned books critically and closely. This gave them a way into the text so that they were more likely to branch out from there and engage the material actively and responsibly on their own—using mnemonic capers.

The more traditional format for teaching such a course might include, on the one hand, many more canonical works and, on the other, a syllabus of less venerated works accompanied by numerous ancillary theoretical readings in politics, psychology, and social history. In either case though, the professor poses as the expert and lectures at the students who, cast in the role of neophytes, take notes on books that they probably have not have read for class and to which they are not likely to return once the course is over. This approach to mastering material barely gives the student a taste of the work being sampled; and even when it does, the taste is not a savory one.

While good arguments can be made for using a hefty anthology, students tend to treat it as just another text-book and often are all too willing to accept unquestioningly the editorial guidelines for interpreting the reading selections. If they own or have access to the complete texts though, and are shown how to apply mnemonic principles when reading them, they are more likely to interact with the entire text on its own terms and come to understand at least selected portions of them from the inside-out. For example, a mind-map like this one can be used to reconstruct every important detail and subtle image from the 9th section of *Beowulf*—details and aural resonances that recur throughout the rest of the epic [FIGURE 1.5].

**Figure 1.5**

Coming up with, using, and applying organizational mnemonics gives students the skills, confidence, and impetus to return to the entire work and to read additional sections, filling in gaps as they go. This applies even to complicated Tudor political allegories like Sackville's *Mirror for Magistrates*, which traces the fall of famous men and women in English history [FIGURE 1.6]. This skeletal caper was given to each student so they could fill in and perhaps illustrate salient points as their

## Figure 1.6

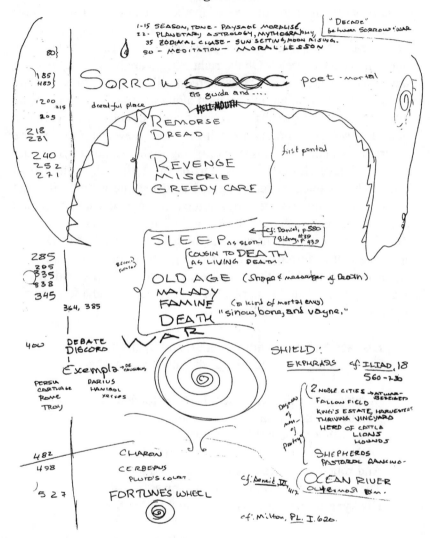

reading of the poem progressed. The caper was a basic pattern, a narrative and symbolic flow-chart, that functioned both as a scorecard (to make sure they were hitting all the right bases as they proceeded) and as a kind of prospective *mind map* (about which more will be said in the next section). This caper gives line numbers on the left-hand margin and the names of characters in the middle according to the order they are encountered once the poet, guided by Sorrow, enters the Underworld, which is represented in this mind map as the "Maw of Hell," or Hellmouth, so familiar to students of medieval and early Tudor literature. Such a gruesome motif works well as the dominant image for organizing a series of sequential points because, insofar as it arrests one's attention, it is easy to recall. On the right margin are listed other notable poetic devices and references encountered as the poem unfolds. By virtue of this way of grouping information along an axis of "line number, character, and poetic devices" the students found themselves with a graphic version of a *memory grid*. As a result they were never at a loss where they were in this poem—and one that, owing to the irregular syntax and complicated image clusters, was by far the most difficult of the works assigned. This enabled students, instead of struggling to find out what was going on or who was speaking, to focus more on the subtle relation between the formal design of the poem and the stunning emblematic images. Take for example the spiral at the bottom, the shield of Death's companion, War (referred to as his "targe"), which spins the reader into a kind of interior world within the already circumscribed world of Hades—an image, incidentally, paralleled to Fortune's wheel a few stanzas later (Sylvester, 1984: 231-32):

> His face forhewed with woundes, and by his side,
> There hunge his targe with gashes depe and wyde.
>
> In mids of which, depaynted there we founde
> Deadly debate, al ful of snaky heare,
> That with a blouddy fillet was ybound.
> Outbreathing nought but discord everywhere.
> And round about were portrad here and there
> The hugie hostes, Darius and his power,
> His kynges, prynces, his pieres, and all his flower.

This part of the caper being completed by everyone, one group was then assigned to use an enlarged and blank shield to represented visually what "depaynted there we founde." Another group was asked to write a narrative description based on what the first group drew, and a third group then commented on faithfulness to and departures from the original text. The extended series of capers led students to a deeper and more thorough understanding of the poem. It also gave them practical ways of understanding the limits and liberties of bringing their modern sensibilities to an older text. Finally students left the poem with knowledge of the moral lessons it set out to teach.

By the same token, they are apt to be positively disposed toward a potentially daunting poem like Dante's *Inferno* if they have ready-made points of access at their disposal [FIGURE 1.7 (Mandelbaum, 1988: 343)]. At least as early as the sixteenth century, schematic charts of Dante's Hell and Paradise were discussed in terms of providing readers with ready-made, convenient sites within an artificial memory theatre (Rossellius, 1579).

When studying vast bodies of material, the essential elements come into focus best once we have found ways to make them stand out. Whether visualizing encoded mnemonics, or marking key words, or highlighting sentences in bright colors, the object initially is to single out so that later you can gather them together and perhaps then compose some version of a "Sum and Substance" document. If the resulting abstract, really more akin to a textual repository, is constructed well, then we can find our way back into the original and move about at will. The trick is (and it bears repeating) for you to be able to have reliable points of access to get back into the original. This is what will enable you to box it up and take it with you. But what then will you do with the box? Simply tie it up neatly with a ribbon and put it on a shelf, and point at it periodically? Or, will you open it up at appropriate intervals and put the contents to novel and exciting uses, perhaps with respect to the contents of other boxes you might have on hand?

During the Renaissance many such metaphorical boxes could be displayed, and thereby contemplated for further applications, by using architectural motifs and theatrical backdrops. For example, book frontispieces recalled the design of way stations in allegorical processions, and typically included mnemonically charged figures each in its proper place or compartment [FIGURE 1.8]. Sometimes frontispieces, like Sir Walter Ralegh's *History of the World*, emblematically rendered the general thematic concerns of a work, rather than giving a systematic display of contents [FIGURE 1.9]. In other cases, however, as in Burton's *Anatomy of Melancholy*, frontispieces were visual epitomes of the entire work reflecting not only the main headings but also the way in which the information was to be delivered [FIGURE 1.10]. Of course once the design was set in your memory, you would have a ready-made way to recall the key movements of the book and thus to find your way back into and within it in the future.

**Figure 1.7**

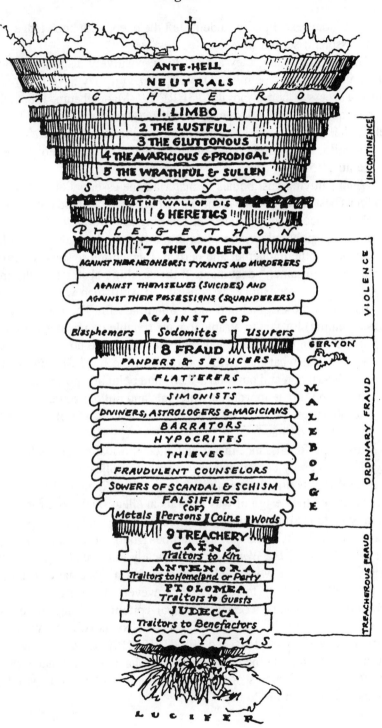

**Figure 1.8**

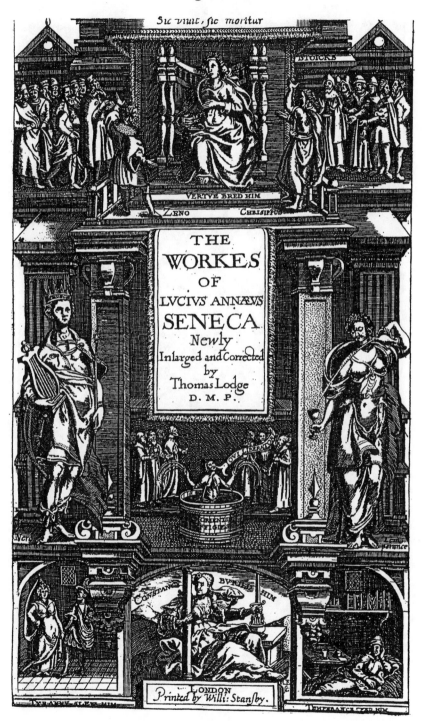

**Figure 1.9**

**Figure 1.10**

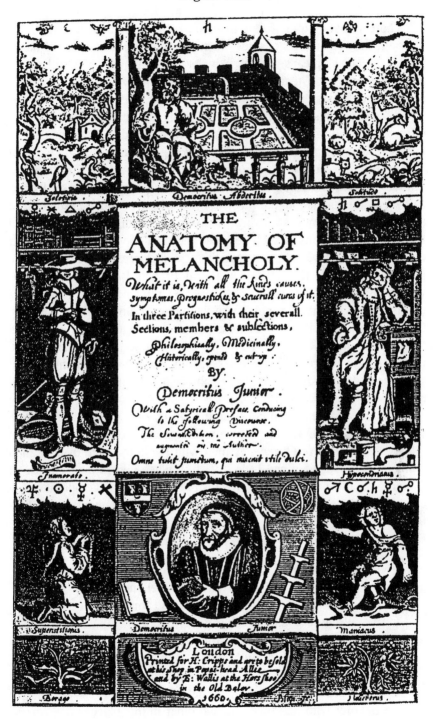

These visual epitomes were likened to abstracted bodies of thought;
after all, the very word "chapter" comes from the Latin *caput* for head,
just as "record" means literally "by heart." Likewise we still speak
about the body of a text with its periodic section *head*ings, which, in
many books today, are *capit*alized. Often encoded mnemonic images
were described and elaborated in easy-to-recall rhymes, in what was
termed "The Mind of the Frontispiece" (Corbett and Lightbown, 1979).
It was typical during the Renaissance to compare the image and word of
mnemonic devices to the body and soul, especially in *imprese*
(Giovio,1559). The better to help my students understand this allegorical way of thinking about our place in the world as a kind of aestheticized
moral allegory, they read several treatises concerning the decorum and
formal considerations of such devices, and then constructed either their
own emblems (addressing universal themes) or *imprese* (expressing more
personal intentions [FIGURE 1.11]). Sir Francis Bacon, for example,
valued such emblematic designs because they reduced "conceits intellectual to images sensible, which strike the memory more" (Bacon, 1605).
One student, Rico Blancaflor, took this to heart when he rendered the
main points in an essay by Bacon in the fluid style of contemporary
illustrated adventure novels ("zines"), thus making the content easy to
construe and reconstruct at a glance, and also remaining true to Bacon's
emblematic ideal [FIGURE 1.12].

The practical lesson in constructing an *impresa* gave my students a
solid foundation for reading densely allegorical works later that term
like Spenser's *Faerie Queene*. Armed with the knowledge of how such
emblems worked, they had little difficulty when confronted with Book
II, canto 9, concerning Sir Guyon's visit to the Castle of Temperance (an
elaborately developed allegory of the body) that is frequently under attack, but which is overseen from within by the sober Lady Alma (the
soul).

> Of all God's works, which do this world adorn,
> > There is no one more fair and excellent,
> > Then is man's body for power and form,
> > While it is kept in sober government;
> > But none than it, more foul and indecent,
> > Distempered through misrule and passions base:
> > It grows a Monster, and incontinent
> > Doth lose his dignity and native grace.
> Behold, who list, both one and other in this place.

**Figure 1.11**

DON'T LET SCHOOL GET IN THE WAY OF
YOUR EDUCATION.

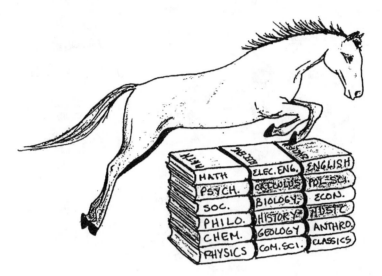

Behold the horse, as a free and wild beast,
It will try to escape confines and fetters:
So there are some that do protest
When forced to learn numbers and letters,
But those who run away from the books and tests
Will only earn scoffs from their peers and their betters.
So look to the horse that accepts what he learns,
He jumps above and beyond and gets what he earns.

# Figure 1.12

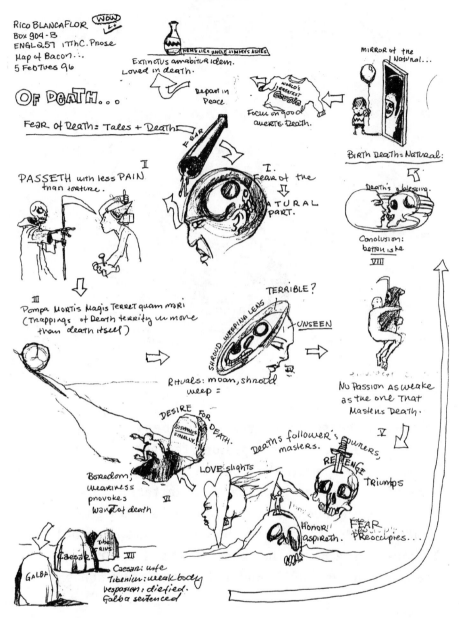

These nine lines, incidentally, were singled out by six students independent of one another when the class was asked to identify a stanza that was the "most emblematic" of Spenser's poetic craft, allegorical project, and literary style. Barring the possibility they read the same secondary source or discussed the poem outside of class, the fact they chose the same stanza over 1,200 assigned that term, indicates to me, as a teacher, there is something here worthy of further investigation—whether about Spenser, about mnemonic tagging, or about how students attend to certain specific features when reading a long and involved poem.

When I teach Spenser in a Survey class each student becomes an expert on at least one assigned canto of *The Faerie Queene* (there are between 40-60 stanzas per canto, and twelve cantos per book). This means they need to know how their canto fits in with the larger design of the book and also with respect to Spenser's over all poetic project. They commit to memory 27 lines (three stanzas) and then use this block of the poem as the basis for both an extemporaneous encomium (laudatory oration) and also a traditional research paper. Intimate knowledge of the specific poetic and rhetorical principles informing and animating the stanzas gives each student personal points of access to the soul of Spenser's work, just as their research provides a view of the larger body of the text. This pattern of study, in general, characterizes the method I use, in conjunction with classroom capers, to get at the aesthetic core of the subject of instruction.

Alexander Ross, who continued Ralegh's *History of the World* (and achieved some notoriety for doing so), spoke of his appended chronology as embodying and depicting the "Soul of Historical Knowledge; wherein, as in a small Map may be seen the chief memorable passages that have fallen out in the world" (Ross, 1652: b4ᵛ). This practice of collapsing information into a point that later could be unpacked of its contents, was central to Renaissance emblematic thinking and it took on a variety of forms. Whether reduced to an entry in a chronological table, an emblem or allegorical figure, an epigram or a proverb, such "small maps" all have one thing in common: they collapse much in little.

As with a poetic image that uses few words to stand for and express a range of feelings, or an *impresa* that ingeniously declares one's professed intention, mnemonic devices are all like germinated seeds which one's wit (like life-giving water) can revive, allow to take root, and grow beyond itself. Andrew Marvell, for example, made this principle of design a theme in his poetry, and the opening lines of "A Drop of Dew" disclose a still more encompassing, and more expansive, philosophy of aesthetics.

> See how the Orient Dew,
> Shed from the Bosom of the Morn
>   Into the blowing Roses,
> Yet careless of its Mansion new,
> For the clear Region where 'twas born,
>   Round itself encloses,
>     And in its little Globe's Extent,
> Frames as it can its native Element.

Our course then is set; let us allow Marvell's image of a drop of dew, like Ross's reference to a small map, to guide us in our quest to learn more about how we can make the most out of the time-tried techniques to consolidate and condense information into luminously charged packets of recoverable—often expandable—meanings. Such mnemonics though, whether they reduce the information to a symbolic idea or image, or to a finely pointed word or epigram, are not merely static devices for recalling previously fixed or determined content. Rather, through the decorous and creative application of the Memory Arts, they become generative and dynamic tools to facilitate lasting, responsible, and artful learning.

Owing to the necessarily interactive nature of working with mnemonically oriented capers, students become more personally engaged with the material and less reliant on the teacher to "make them learn." As a consequence they take a more responsible role in what they are learning. This in turn enables students, as a culminating aspect of working reflectively with artificial memory systems, to focus attention toward the deliberate cultivation of their character with an eye toward perfecting their moral conduct.

The ethical claim that I am making here reaches much farther than did my previous somewhat more modest academic one, which Mary Carruthers characterized as follows: "'Mnemonic criticism' is not one 'approach' among many to the *interpretation* of literature (as Engel's term might imply) but was a fundamental feature of ancient and medieval art, since it was basic both to elementary pedagogy and to all meditative composition" (Carruthers, 1992: 103). To this I would add that mnemonic criticism not only was *but also still can be* a fundamental feature of learning and an integral step on the path toward ethical development. I contend that mnemonics are not just a *technique* (a tool for thinking and inventing), but also a spur to conscience which gets one moving along a path toward more reflective and humane dealings in the world.

# II. Five Main Types

This section covers a practical five-point program for using generative mnemonics. As such, it presents a more systematic approach to the general ideas introduced in the previous section. Learning more about how to come up with and implement memory images has the added benefit of inspiring us to be more creative and responsible in our interpretation and manipulation of symbols—whether in books or the world. The five main mnemonic practices I have adapted for classroom use are (1) Tagging, (2) Memory Grids, (3) Mind Mapping, (4) Magic Circles, and (5) Speaking Pictures.

For the sake of making them easier to recall and use I have devised a simple hand mnemonic, which incidentally models what will be described in what follows [FIGURE 1.13]. Each type can stand on its own; and yet, taken collectively from thumb to fifth finger, constitutes a flesh-and-blood tool for manipulating points of information with which we then can build something original. Since each organizes information in different ways, the properties of each type must be respected when being used. Because the range and variety of such capers is vast indeed, I have had to confine myself to only a few examples of each main type. When devising capers for your own ends though, remember you are limited only by the zodiac of your wit.

## 1. Tagging

On our hand mnemonic [FIGURE 1.13], tagging is represented as a cipher composed of the first two letters of the word with an arrow-flourish indicating that more is to follow—literally and figuratively. Tagging is the most rudimentary mnemonic process upon which the others often depend. Tagging is the marking of a designated "place" as being part of one's own intellectual territory, a landmark one wants to indicate as having been visited. In this sense it is like the old motto "Kilroy was

**Figure 1.13**

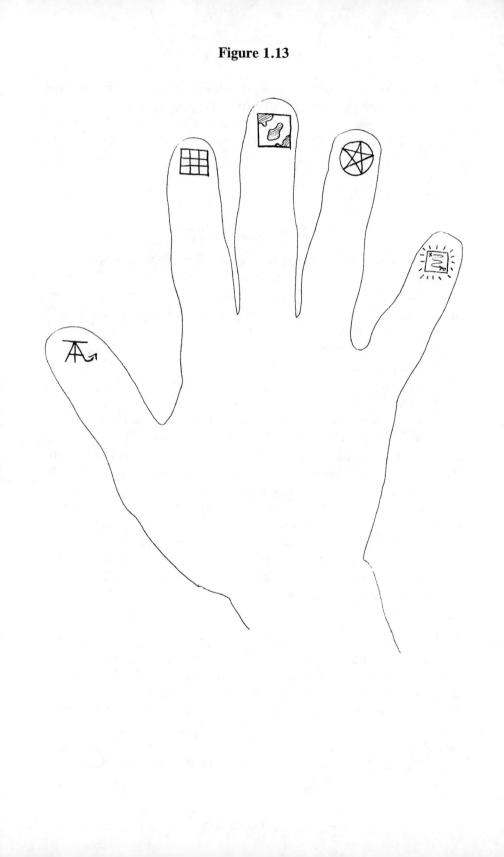

here" left by U.S. servicemen abroad, or like the more up-to-date spray-painted ciphers on urban walls and overpasses. Like these personal marks made on public property, mnemonic tags become part of one's own internal repertoire, and can be taken to signify larger social meanings beyond what originally may have been intended. Street tagging turns one's environment into a virtual memory theatre, remarkable for the places visited and the common public spaces that have, in a sense, become part of the tagger's territory covered, his or her graphically claimed property. Academic tagging on classroom capers works in the other direction: it is geared to create a kind of interior landscape within which tell-tale guideposts help students to identify, and thereby make their own, key dates, facts, lines of poetry—the bare bones of future learning. The use value of such commonplace information, which can be thought of as intellectual capital, extends beyond its having been marked as being something worthy of finding a place in one's table-book. If it simply is stored away and never used, then it is like congealed capital, which serves no social purpose and accumulates nothing beyond itself—like the dragon's treasure horde in *Beowulf*. So too tagged words, like discrete jewels stored in a treasury, stand ready to be selected and placed in a new setting—a point lodged in the word thesaurus. So long as tagged words are seen as being part of a larger literary economy, then, like capital that is wisely invested or property put to a good use, they are likely to yield great profit.

Tagging can, though it need not always, take the form of reducing words or ideas to cryptic symbols that stand for them. Appropriate tag-devices can suggest themselves from within the work itself (for example, the number 1 for Una in Spenser's *Faerie Queene*, a star for Stella in Sidney's sonnet cycle), or mnemonic place-holders might just as easily come from the tagger's own private set of memory images (the works of Blake and Rimbaud, for example, contain many such idiosyncratically coded emblems whose meanings unfold the more one reads of those authors). Fundamental to tagging though is that first one must identify key concepts or words to be tagged, perhaps grouped topically, so they can be seen both in their own right and also as part of a larger constellation of points constituting much wider meanings.

For example one caper, which while introducing students to working with tag words, was designed primarily to help them learn to recite the opening lines of Chaucer's *Canterbury Tales* and to do so with some degree of fluency, with some knowledge of and respect for the original language, with basic comprehension of the semantic sense of the passage, and with rudimentary knowledge of the rhetorical and poetic conventions in which it was written [FIGURE 1.14]. Because of the nature of the passage selected, this caper also helped to clarify for the students the plan of the entire work, to fix in their minds the basic poetic form and meter, and to bring to prominence issues of social class (*condicioun* and *degree*; "S" and "T" on the right).

Being able to recite the words though, while a worthwhile exercise in and of itself, is only the beginning of the adventure. For as Montaigne admonished: "The gain from our study is to have become better and wiser by it. . . . To know by heart is not to know; it is to retain what we have given our memory to keep" (Montaigne, *Essays*, I.26: 112). And so I instructed the students first to try to learn the lines on their own; then, while working in groups in class, I asked them to fill in the blanks of the caper and to focus on (and enter into their notebooks) any patterns that emerged from the tagged words. Among some of the things they discovered and thereby kept for their own, which then could be reserved for future use (certainly more so than had I adopted the "lecture-listen" model of instruction), were the following main points.

First, most students noticed at a glance that the poem rhymed in couplets, and a few who had had prior training concluded that the meter was iambic pentameter. "What rhymes with *soote*?" one student asked another about "C" so that her answer-sheet would be complete by the end of the class period. Also, by virtue of knowing that couplets were a regulating influence on the poem, the more attentive students noticed that *a line was missing* from the text as typed on the caper sheet (the correct couplet should read: "And palmers for to seeken straunge strondes, / To ferne halwes, couthe in soundry londes"). They scored bonus points by bringing this to the attention of the teacher who, from the start of the course, had urged students to be alert to the fallibility, no less than the puzzling and playful aspects of some texts (and some teachers), then as now. What is more, once this "missing line" was brought to their attention, they were less likely to forget the key terms and images that this couplet communicated about the longing to seek "strange shores and far-off shrines known in various lands." Another main point they learned was that Chaucer used recognizable classical poetic conventions (his reference to the wind as "Zephyrus" and allusion to Aries as "the Ram"). They also noticed that a commonplace rhetorical structure guides and constrains how we are to construe and understand what seems to flow

**Figure 1.14**

*Canterbury Tales*, "General Prologue," lines 1-42

{ A } that { B } with his shoures soote
The droghte of March hath perced to the { C },
And bathed every veyne in swich licour,
Of which vertu engendred is the { D },
{ E } Zephyrus eek with his sweete breeth
Inspired hath in every holt and heeth
The tendre croppes, and the younge { F }
Hath in the Ram his halve cours yronne,
And smale fowles maken melodye
That sleepen al the night with open yë—
So priketh hem Nature in hir corages—
{ G } longen folk to goon on { H },
And palmeres for to seeken straunge londes;
And specially from every shires ende
Of Engelond to { I } they wende,
The hooly blisful martir for to seke
That hem hath holpen whan that they were seeke.
  Bifel that in that seson on a day,
In Southwerk at the { J } as I lay,
Redy to wenden on my { K }
To { L } with ful devout corage,
At nyght was come into that hostelrye
Wel { M } and { N } in a compaignye
Of sondry folk, by aventure yfalle
In felaweshipe, and pilgrimes were they alle
That toward { O } wolden ryde.
The chambres and the stables weren wide,
And wel we were esed at the beste.
And shortly, whan the { P } was to reste,
So hadde I spoken with hem everichoon
That I was of hir { Q } anon,
And made forward erly for to ryse,
To take oure way ther as I yow { R }.
  But nathelees, whil I have tyme and space,
Er that I ferther in this tale pace,
Me thinketh it accordaunt to resoun
To telle you al the { S }
Of eech of hem, so as it seemed me,
And which they were, and of what { T },
And eek in what array that they were inne:
And at a { U } than wol I first bigynne.

A  *Whan (When)*
B  *Aprill*
C  *roote*
D  *flour*
E  *Whan (when)*
F  *sonne (sun)*
G  *Thanne (Then)*
H  *pilgrimages*
I  *Caunterbury*
J  *Tabard*
K  *pilgrimage*
L  *Caunterbury*
M  *nyne*
N  *twenty*
O  *Caunterbury*
P  *sonne (sun)*
Q  *felawship*
R  *devyse*
S  *condicioun*
T  *degree*
U  *knyght*

conversationally from the speaker's poetic reflections of what happened "in that seson on a day" (the "when, when, then" formula comes into view when students attend closely to "A," "E, and "G"); by the same token, a student who wanted to pursue the implications of a possible pun on sun/son ("F" and "P") observed that "something is going on with seasons and cycles of time and the idea of rebirth—maybe resurrection?" In the end, information concerning the rhyme scheme, poetic conventions, and rhetorical structure like that just described, can be arranged and used in any of a number of ways depending on the special talents of students, the tasks assigned, or uses projected. Whether or not you are a teacher or student of literature, it is my hope that you can find ways of applying these principles to your areas of endeavor.

## 2. Memory Grids

Memory grids allow you to box up minimal, though often highly suggestive, bits of already tagged information. But more than this, by virtue of the way memory grid capers are set up (and this is where the professorial hand can show itself to its best advantage), they tend to encourage the generation, and not just the storage, of basic information. Instead of recalling unchanging facts that fit into neat segments of orderly arranged boxes (as is the case with the Periodic Table of Elements) or filling in the blanks with answers that implacably reflect a predictable pattern (as with multiplication tables), the students, often working in groups, were asked to come up with appropriate responses and then to express them as "mnememes" (Martin, 1979: 55). This meant that students first had to locate, and then tag, the information. Once it was secured and set off on its own, the students then could regard it carefully and critically so as to determine and decide how it might be used most effectively, appropriately, and responsibly (effectively, with respect to the student's goals and aims; appropriately, with respect to the course requirements and institutional guidelines; and responsibly, with respect to the integrity of the work being studied).

This process comes into focus, for example, on a rudimentary memory grid caper from a Renaissance drama class, in which students were given just a list of characters from two of the assigned plays (Shalani Goel's responses are given in italics) [FIGURE 1.15]. As this was among the first capers of the term, it was designed in part to help convey the sorts of things they should begin to be looking for on their own so that, as the

**Figure 1.15**

(1)

| character | from | how died | citation |
|---|---|---|---|
| Tamberlaine | *Scythia* | *sickness, ironically from a cut he made* | *5.3.248* |
| Zenocrate | *Egypt* | *sickness, consumptive* | *2.4.95* |
| the virgins | *Damascus* | *slaughtered by Tam's men; corpses hoisted* | *5.1.120-31* |
| Calyphus | *Persia* | *stabbed by his leader/father, Tamberlaine* | *4.1.120* |
| Bajazeth | *Turkey* | *bashes brains against inside of his cage* | *5.1.301-03* |
| Zerbina | *Turkey* | *bashes brains on outside of husband's cage* | *5.1.316-18* |
| Olympia | *Balsera* | *tricks Theridamas to stab her in the neck* | *4.2.81* |
| Gorboduc | *Britain* | *slain by populace* | *between 4 & 5* |
| Videna | *Britain* | *slain by populace* | *between 4 & 5* |
| Ferrex | *Britain* | *killed by brother, Porrex out of insecurity* | *3.1.941-45* |
| Porrex | *Britain* | *killed by his mother, Videna to avenge son* | *4.2.140-44* |

(2) Compare and contrast the issue of succession by looking at specific topics, play to play:

| II Tamberlaine | Gorboduc |
|---|---|
| *sons and followers are not as willing or eager to rule and take charge as Tam has done (esp. Calyphus)* | *sons are not trained to rule effectively and hear counsel of often incompetent advisors; like the father in that they ignore good advice and don't know it* |
| *he has but one kingdom and two sons to succeed (after discounting the third as a coward) and wants there to be only one ruler* | *by splitting kingdom among two sons in effort to be fair, he sparks civil war b/c each is jealous of the other's share* |
| *his sons will never be able to fill his shoes as a great conqueror; don't have his natural abilities or his charmed skin (and astral destiny)* | *Gorboduc tries to retire too early and sons cannot safe-guard the stability of the once unified kingdom* |
| *How much loyalty can exist among members of the family if the loftiest goal is an earthly crown (given to Amydas)?* | *b/c Gorboduc didn't give the kingdom in entirety to oldest son and b/c wife was Partial to Ferrex, bad blood was bred* |

course progressed and the material got more complicated, they would need minimal professorial guidance when constructing their own capers. One student reflected that distilling detailed responses into manageable "mnemic-bites" (strictly verbal expressions of mnememes) helped her make her own, as it were, discrete parts of a larger whole, which she could then fit into a more encompassing scheme still (as can be seen from this caper covering a whole semester's assignments [FIGURE 1.16], which bears comparison to FIGURE 1.4 from the same course).

These slots cannot (and are not intended to) hold much. The student must come up with direct and concise tags that stand in for, and trigger recollection of, key aspects of the works being studied. For example, the narrative thread of Skelton's "The Tunnyng of Elynour Rummyng" is summed up well (under Sk. "El." on the memory grid): "tells of a woman who makes good beer and people give anything to drink it." Just below this entry, the student has listed as "something else true and accurate" a moral theme that she took from the poem: "Intemperance to trade things in order to indulge."

The poem's structure and meaning obviously are far more complex than an undergraduate's synopsis can allow; still, her tagged findings hit quite close to what one of the greatest contemporary explicators of Skelton has related. The student's moral "mnemic-bite" accorded well with Arthur Kinney's parting assessment of the poem as "a sermon fit for every age" (Kinney, 1987: 187). By such means, whether or not they are aware of the research by experts, students can begin to build an edifice of knowledge out of the bare bones encountered in their studies. Along the way they can recognize and seek to emulate traits associated with the attempt to live honorably and thus to shun those that lead to dissipation and desecration.

## 3. Mind Mapping

Mind Mapping helps students flesh out what memory grids can only intimate through tagged mnememes. Mind maps help students visually track the flow of thoughts—whether their own or those of others (Margulies, 1991). This technique, once perfected on paper, enables the student to keep in mind a sequence of narrative events or complicated shifts in ideas. For example, we see its practical benefits in a schematic chart used for identifying the succession of straightforward events in the Morality Play *Everyman* (which, incidentally, follows a stark chiastic plan) [FIGURE 1.17] (Cf. Nänny, 1987: 75-97). Mind mapping also can make use of artificial memory images to record and display key points extracted from still more complicated works, like John Skelton's satirical *Bouge of Court* [FIGURE 1.18]. Moreover, this particular form

**Figure 1.16**

| | Beowulf | CT, Ind, Bou | SPENSER | Sidney | Sh LLL | Sk. "El" | H&L, WYATT, SURREY |
|---|---|---|---|---|---|---|---|
| subjectively rank by - + | + | -, +, + | + | + | + | SKELTON | — |
| title & dating; author's name | "Beowulf" (650-850) author? | CT "Conquest" (1380) Ind+Sackville=Bowkdton(?) | Faerie Queen Edmund Spenser (1596) | Astrophil & Stella" Phillip Sidney (1554) | Love's Labor Lost Shakespeare (1564-?) | Bowge of Elynour Rummyng (~1500) | H&L Marlowe(?) Wyatt (1503?) Surrey (1517?) |
| genre; kind of work it is; models... | epic poem from Middle ages; most likely was from oral tradition; no known models. | poems that tell stories; idealized in a quest; pagan, biblical images modified after Ariosto, Tasso, Virgil, esp. ди Beowull | allegorical poem; epic + a romance; full of numerous... Antiochijur; inspired by classical works. | Allegorical sonnet + fold allegorical pattern; that has a simple sequence of events; allegorical | romance, comedy + tragedy; play that was inspired by Spenser | rhyme scheme aa, bbcc... "Skeltonic" | H&L is a "mini epic" and a tragic love story; Wyatt + Sur write about love that was not been awarded to them |
| characteristic features of style, tropes | Caesura throughout, a lot of kennings, epithets, some litotes. | | A line-action—lambic pentameter; sestet-iambic pentameter. | many conceits, emblems, though lit images. → for Sidney | Constant rhyme scheme in dialogue. | specific images | Surrey invented blank verse & English sonnet |
| content summed and its place in the sweep of ENGL lit & cultural success | A quest to conquer over Grendel & two monsters; the quest is read by Beowulf, the hero. An early epic w/ valiant battles. | All three works are narrated stories that are full of an event or events that are active w/ a moral in their ending. | Quest of Guyon to obtain the 12 virtues that make a gentleman. Spenser's intention was to present the 12 virtues in 12 books through the use of allegory. | Astrophil professing his love to Stella. A step trajectory of wooing a poem that involves wooing, desire, virtue + passion. Founder of love sonnets. | 3 women tease the 3 men who are wooing them. In the end, they accept their love but will not be together. Comical, dramatic plays. | tells of a woman who has a good beer & give anything to drink it | All of these poems discuss the trauma of wooing someone and trying to gain their love. Also learns to suffer through & gaining this love |
| something else true & accurate | Great value placed on Kinship; stresses loyalty vs. incurring expenditure; reversal of fortune, desire for fame. | Similar poetic qualities in all 3 authors. Offer morals or virtues to redeem spirit. | Book II deals directly with the virtue of temperance (how much someone can be intemperate. | Based on how Sidney felt about Penelope Rich, a woman who would never return his love. | Common theme of Shakespeare—the wisdom of the foolish vs. the foolishness of the wise. | Intemperance to trade things in order to indulge. | The narrative quality of H&L; the other 2 poets relay more personal feeling through a poetic form that helps reflect them. |
| summed up | Great epic qualities; poetic diction is difficult but beautiful. | Narratives are entertaining with some humor and imagination. | An intricate allegory with detailed symbolic descriptions. Very beautiful poetic diction. | Passionate sonnets. Many reoccurring thought images. Very emblematic. | Excellent example of Shakespeare's plots & the themes represented in them. | Allegorical images to depict detailed story line. | Speak of a strong passion of love that the pain it can cause. |

# Figure 1.17

Mind Map of *Everyman*

focal metaphor is the account book (reckoning); "telling" (counting / recounting)

HOMO VIATOR -- Life as Pilgrimage

MESSENGER                                                          DOCTOR

GOD                                                          ANGEL

DEATH                                          GOOD   DEEDS

7 VICES                                    7 SACRAMENTS

FELLOWSHIP                          DISCRETION,
comes & goes                        STRENGTH,
                                    5 WITS,
                                    BEAUTY -- all depart

COUSIN                          KNOWLEDGE &
& KINDRED                        CONFESSION

GOODS                     GOOD DEEDS
on the ground             start where you are

final FALL        begin RECOVERY

(pivot)

**Figure 1.18**

MIND MAP OF SKELTON'S <u>BOUGE OF COURT</u>

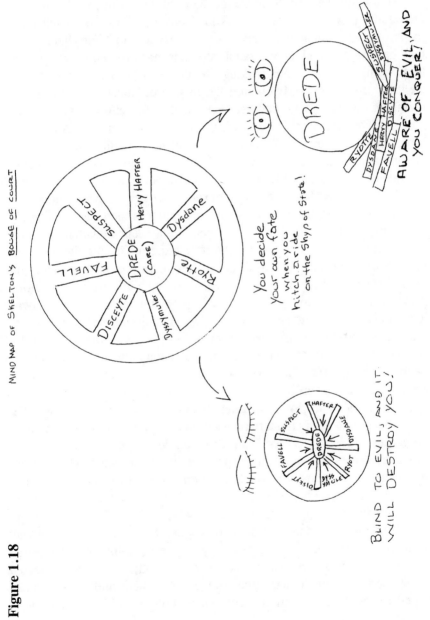

of mnemonic caper can be used as a kind of road map, highlighting, for example, the main allegorical locations and events in an epic—as can be seen here regarding the quest of Sir Guyon, Spenser's Knight of Temperance [FIGURE 1.19] (Cf. Røstvig, 1994: 312-58).

Although a case can be made for the virtues of losing oneself in what one reads, this can be treacherous in Spenser's world. By using mind maps, though, students are less likely to get lost in "Fairyland" once they have tagged and incorporated into their maps key episodes encountered along the way—thus making literal use of "places" from the ancient Art of Memory. My claim is hardly unique; indeed, the plotting of a graphic itinerary historically has been absolutely central to visual mnemonics. This explains, in part, why I chose mind mapping as the third type discussed, corresponding to the centermost, middle, finger that is slightly above and coming between—and yet serving to connect—all of the others [FIGURE 1.13]. From the Renaissance on, mind maps were provided for books like Bunyan's *Pilgrim's Progress*, like one aptly titled "Plan of the Road from the City of Destruction to the Celestial City."

Thus, remaining faithful to the principles associated with these kinds of mnemonic exercises though simplifying and modifying them for the classroom, students are able to descry and map out even the most involved patterns of thought, like those for example in Burton's sprawling *Anatomy of Melancholy* [FIGURE 1.20]. The student here (obviously an accomplished illustrator) has selected a contemporary image to designate the stultifying culmination of idleness—T.V. And were Burton living today, he too would warn us about television, situated at the end of a deadly domino-effect, as a way to emblematize in a succinct memory image the main point of his section on cures for melancholy: "be not solitary; be not idle." What Richard Feynman did to clarify some especially dense patches in modern physics using his revolutionary diagrams, an earnest student like Rico Blancaflor can do to some especially dense passages in seventeenth-century prose using his graphic wit. For example the crutch shown in connection with the Eucharist faithfully sums up in a strikingly vivid memory image the crux of Burton's argument and attitude regarding cures for melancholy.

Mind mapping is a heuristic, pedagogical, tool. It is an effective way to depict rudimentary and suggestively disclosive points of reference so that a larger structure can be reconstituted, and so that then selected twists and turns of the narrative, as well as broader and more complicated issues, themes, and concepts—including ethical considerations—

**Figure 1.19**

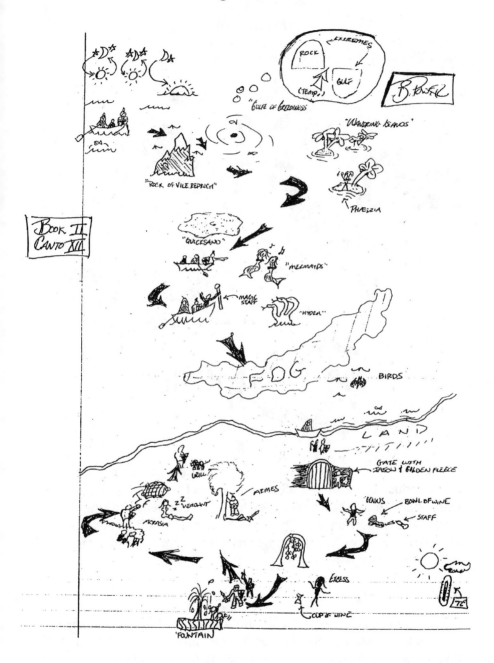

**Figure 1.20**

Anatomy of Melancholy [Mem II . subs. vi and conclusions (cure of Despair)].

can be filled in and explored further. This is what I had in mind when, in the introductory section, I alluded to Ezekiel's parable of dry bones being made to live again once they had been covered with sinews and flesh and then were animated by a special kind of breath (in this case, by the Art of Memory). This seemingly miraculous change leads us into the next form of mnemonic capering.

## 4. Magic Circles

Magic Circles enable students to identify and generate connections among, for example, sixteen poets. Such an exercise might very well begin with a variation on a typical memory grid, where the poets are paired so that students can focus on alternative, though still somewhat linear, modes of categorizing and tagging the basic data [FIGURE 1.21]. Students are

## Figure 1.21

| | a key date | gender, religion, ethnicity nationality, sexual preference | points of connection; why are they paired? | something that marks poems; characteristic |
|---|---|---|---|---|
| Hardy | | | | |
| Tennyson | | | | |
| Vaughan | | | | |
| cummings | | | | |
| Larkin | | | | |
| Snyder | | | | |
| Hughes | | | | |
| Plath | | | | |
| Atwood | | | | |
| Swenson | | | | |
| Randall | | | | |
| Aiken | | | | |
| Lovelace | | | | |
| Moore | | | | |
| Hopkins | | | | |
| Donne | | | | |

told that such a brief summing up of characteristics (like gender, religion, ethnicity, nationality, sexual preference) must be subjected to further critical examination. Accordingly they were asked to question and discuss whether and the extent to which such categories could help them understand and interpret the poetry. As with every caper assignment, students are encouraged to reflect on how it elicits (and obviates) certain kinds of information by virtue of how it is set up.

Looking beyond the pairing of poets to more open-ended possibilities, the memory grid exercise paved the way for a magic circle caper
[FIGURE 1.22]. This particular diagram is but one of several handed in
that term, as each student charted out some basic connections (often
which reflected work carried out individually on an assigned poet), and
did so on a clear transparency using a colored marker. When different
groups of students were brought together to discuss their findings, the
transparencies were placed one atop the other and projected onto a wall,
which made for lively and informed discussions.

## Figure 1.22

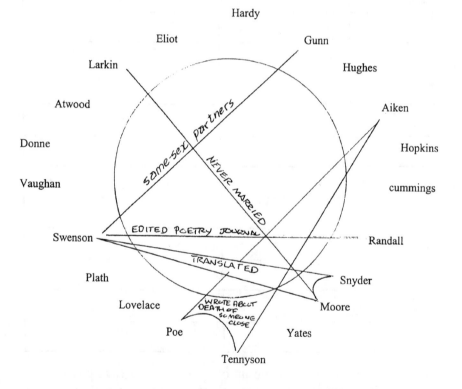

Collaborative learning exercises (both inside and outside the classroom), student reports (based on tutorials, so as to minimize the prolif-
eration of misinformation and factual errors), and recitations (at least
thirty lines per student) took the place of lecturing. Students thus came
to rely on one another, since everyone was responsible for all sixteen of

the poets by the end of term. By pooling their information, the students came to see and to forge links that made lasting and strong impressions. Magic circle capers like this one encourage students to arrange information in evocative ways and to generate questions they might not otherwise have considered.

Preliminary memory grids help students construct their own magic circles, as can be seen for example in this one which situated Kerouac's *On the Road* with respect to other works involving the theme of life being a journey [FIGURE 1.23]. This memory grid made it easy for students to get down some basic points about the works being consid-

## Figure 1.23

Below the names of each *On the Road* character, analyze for puns and allegorical significance; then chart out how they are like or unlike the main wanderers in:

| On the Road | Zarathustra | Winter Journey | Werther |
|---|---|---|---|
| Salvador Paradise | | | |
| Dean Moriarty | | | |
| Carlo Marx | | | |

| | children/wives/lovers | source of income | where is "home"? | habits/tics |
|---|---|---|---|---|
| Sal | | | | |
| Dean | | | | |

ered, and then to arrange, cross-apply, and transfer the information so as to put it to other uses [FIGURE 1.24]. The resulting analytical papers indicated that most students were beginning to discern for themselves some of the larger connections, rifts, and shifts in literary and cultural history in the West.

**Figure 1.24**

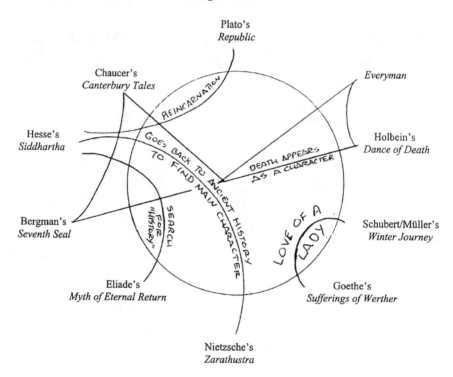

## 5. Speaking Pictures

An entire course of study and whole doctrines of thought can be represented through a series of symbolic images, perhaps paintings or statues in niches, thus turning a room into a virtual Memory Theatre. Such allegorical programs regularly adorned the reception halls, salons, and grand gardens of Renaissance princes. Memory Theatres could take many forms, including triumphal arches, houses of worship, guildhalls, and even inns. There were other kinds of mnemonic "place systems," as they were called, but the commonest was the architectural design (Yates, 1978). The age-old practice of giving elaborate, often poetic, descriptions of the specific symbolic points that previously had been encoded into a picture derives from an age-old rhetorical commonplace known as *ekphrasis* (Bath, 1994; Hulse, 1990).

One semester, for example, I began the course by letting students come up with rudimentary pictures, based on what they already knew, about each of the assigned books: *Daphnis and Chloe, Iliad, Odyssey, Aeneid, Divine Comedy, Decameron, Pantagruel, Don Quixote,* Sophocles's *Antigone* and Marlowe's *Doctor Faustus* [FIGURE 1.25]. As they read the books and became more familiar with them, a few images, or encoded mnemonics, were added at the beginning of each class session. First in their notebooks, and then as a class exercise on the board, students were asked to mark, or tag, the panels in some meaningful way so as to nuance and represent their evolving relationship to and on-going engagement with the books. To help students become familiar with the practical applications of speaking pictures, the first book they read that term was *Daphnis and Chloe*, which begins:

> When I was hunting in Lesbos, I saw, in a wood sacred to the Nymphs, the most beautiful thing I have ever seen—a painting that told a love story. . . . After gazing admiringly at many other scenes, all of a romantic nature, I was seized by a longing to write a verbal equivalent to the painting. So I found someone to explain the picture to me, and composed a work . . . to refresh the memory of those who have been in love and educate those who have not (Longus, 1989: 17).

Accordingly the first caper required that the students make a picture of what the "painting that told a love story" might have looked like. In this way each student kept a running visual record of key episodes in the book, and in so doing came to understand how speaking pictures could give coherence to what one encountered in a book or in the world.

At the end of the term students were asked, by way of a final exam, to reconstruct as much of the panels as would be useful for filling in a memory grid with academic bare bones (author, genre, date, main themes, helpful secondary criticism and how it helped) so that they then could expatiate judiciously on three of the assigned books, each in its own right and also with respect to the others. According to the evaluative criteria used for assessing and measuring the instructional objectives of this particular class, the students exceeded what was expected (including

**Figure 1.25**

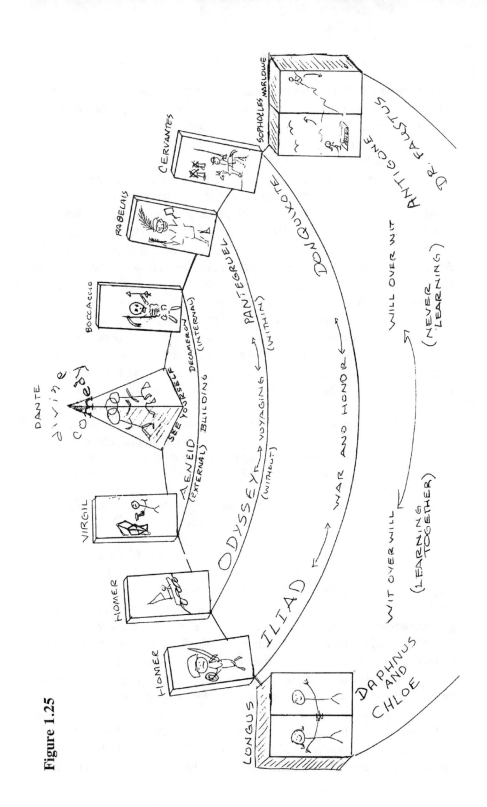

a special-needs pupil who in previous classes, I subsequently learned, had had only marginal success on exams covering a vast body of information). Moreover, the structure of the three-part exam helped students reflect on how information gets stored and recycled. Insofar as students were able to draw on and apply information from one part of the exam to the others thus duplicating information, it could perhaps be deemed a flawed exercise by conventional assessment standards. And yet the form of repetition favored by practical mnemonics served students well as a point of departure; it enabled them to get down what they knew and to do so in a variety of ways, and then to translate and transform that information into something else again.

For example, Part One of the exam, through a standard matching exercise, asked the students to link names and deeds—all of which echoed a dominant theme of our class discussions, human relations. (In the final weeks of class, students presented research projects elucidating how their chosen topic wove its way through three of the books; some reported on the role women, some on guest-host relationships, some on piracy in the Mediterranean world). To help the students do something practical with the "mnemic bites," and in the process to consolidate and situate their knowledge of the facts at hand, they were asked in Part Two (which also had sections on the speaking picture panels and the memory grid) to fill in blanks on family trees. Some of the names from this section could be read back into Part One (the matching exercise) and could feed into Part Three (the original composition). This enabled students to demonstrate the extent to which many "old bones" when carefully excavated and cleaned up made possible a new arrangement of the body of knowledge which, once animated by the Art of Memory, could then take on a new form (whether, for example, an analytical essay or, as one student boldly attempted, an allegorical short story with modern parallels to the three classical epics [see again FIGURE 1.25, left side]).

In another course (one covering benchmark works in English Literature from *Beowulf* to *Paradise Lost*), students created their own speaking picture as part of their final projects. They were assigned to use a shield as the organization mnemonic background image, some precedents for which they had encountered, among other places, in Sackville's "Induction" to *A Mirror for Magistrates* (War's "targe . . . In mids of which depaynted there we founde . . ." [see again FIGURE 1.6]), Spenser's *Fairie Queene*, and of course in the emblematic sonnets of Sidney and in the heraldic allusions riddling the lyrics of Wyatt and

Surrey. In effect, the student's shield could serve as a visual epitome of the course [FIGURE 1.26].

Moving from the top left and then down, I would draw special attention to this rendering of Chaucer's "Pardoner's Tale," where the root of the tree (under which death, in the tale, waits for the rash youths) serves as a figure in a rebus that echoes the cleric's signature refrain: "Therefore my theme is yet, and ever was '*Radix malorum est cupiditas*'" (translated on the student's shield as "$ is the root of evil"). Not every student sought to intertwine various types of mnemonics into this project as did Britt Farwick, though most like her followed some sort of a sequential itinerary. Irrespective of what approach or combination of approaches was chosen though, all of them demonstrated the extent to which the students had taken to heart what was covered during the term and made of it, literally and allegorically, something they could carry away with them from the course—to help ward off Oblivion—as they went out into the world.

The guiding theme that term was temperance, and it was accompanied by the *sententia* "Bene legere saecla vincere [To read well is to master the ages]." One student depicted the course motto as a living vine twisting its way through the main terms encountered that semester, ingeniously arranged as tag words mnemonically linked to the letters in "TEMPERANCE" (the original shield was color-coded as well) [FIGURE 1.27]. It was a happy coincidence indeed that the noppy "ale" in Skelton's "Elynour Rummyng" preceded "anagogical" in her list; reveling "Comus," seductive "Circe," and "chaos" appeared in close proximity—something all of us would do well to keep in mind, but college students especially. By virtue of pursuing this mnemonic scheme, one which required that she look back at her notes and re-read parts of the assigned books so as to identify and cull appropriate tag words, this student postulated and defended some remarkable connections between developments in English literature and Augustinian theology in her final essay.

But irrespective of what thesis was or was not fully evinced in a paper crowning a semester of work, the practical knowledge of mnemonic capering itself, seen and used as a viable and fundamental approach to literature and life—coupled with the moral messages one encountered along the way—was a fine and noble thing for students to have gotten out of a course required of all English majors [FIGURE 1.28]. For it is by these means that we are more likely to learn to see that at

**Figure 1.26**

**Figure 1.27**

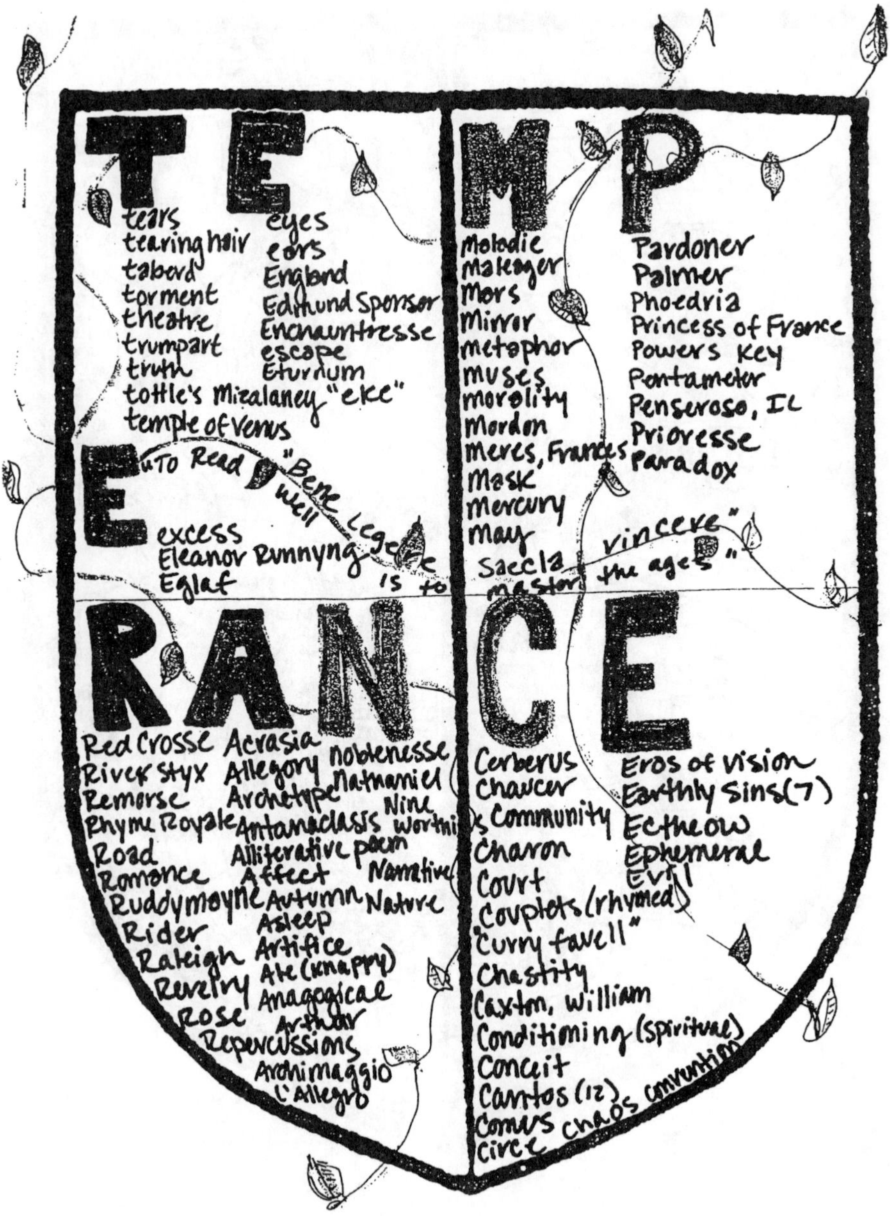

TEMPERANCE

tears — eyes
tearing hair — ears
tabard — England
torment — Edmund Sponsor
theatre — Enchauntresse
trumpart — escape
truth — Eterdum
tottle's Mizalaney "eke"
temple of Venus

"To Read" "Bene Legere"
well

excess
Eleanor Runnyng is to
Eglaf master the ages"

Melodie — Pardoner
makeager — Palmer
mors — Phoedria
mirror — Princess of France
metaphor — Powers Key
muses — Pentameter
morality — Penseroso, IL
Mordon — Prioresse
Meres, Frances — Paradox
Mask
Mercury
May
Saecla "vincere"

Red Crosse — Acrasia
River Styx — Allegory — Noblenesse
Remorse — Archetype — Nathaniel
Rhyme Royale — Antanaclasis — Nine
Road — Alliterative poem — Worthi
Romance — Affect — Narrative
Ruddymoyne — Autumn — Nature
Rider — Asleep
Raleigh — Artifice
Revelry — Ate (knappy)
Rose — Anagogical
Repercussions — Arthur
Archimaggio
L'Allegro

Cerberus — Eros of Vision
Chaucer — Earthly Sins (7)
Community — Ectheow
Charon — Ephemeral
Court — Evil
Couplets (rhymed)
"Curry favell"
Chastity
Caxton, William
Conditioning (Spiritual)
Conceit
Cantos (12)
Comus chaos convention
Circe

**Figure 1.28**

times we are not only like, but, each in our own ways, we *are* Sir Guyon, the Knight of Temperance, and he us. By the same token, since at times we are likely to find ourselves deeply implicated in Burton's discourse on despair, let us hope as well that at times we can be like—and indeed can *be*—Everyman, to whom Knowledge says: "I will go with thee, and be thy guide, / In thy most need to go by thy side."

# III. Moving On

Through my teaching I have sought to make available a variety of time-tried mnemonic techniques as a preliminary step toward finding authentic points of connection to works of literature, art, and philosophy. It has been my experience that students trained to be adept at inventing and applying mnemonics tend to carry with them, not only the specific target-skills (close reading, analytical thinking, cogent writing) and the designated content (for example, Book II of Spenser's *Faerie Queene*), but also the larger moral themes (like the active quest for practical temperance). By virtue of the mnemonic capers that students were assigned, which cumulatively constituted a visual record of their journey toward Knowledge, they succeeded in internalizing, each in their own ways, reminders of the moral guideposts discovered in great books that then could be applied in their own lives and given new applications in the world.

Everyone wins when we encourage students to keep in mind what they should be able to do with what they are learning. Like a visual artist, actor, or musician, they learn to look upon their work as a performance, even as they strive to acquire the skills needed to perform effectively, appropriately, and responsibly. Recognizing that it is not the process of learning or the student's effort that teachers can assess and grade, mnemonic capers need to take into account the evaluative aspect of a finished "work-product." With this in mind in the chapters that follow, we will look more closely at the critical and analytical aspects, as well as at the creative and peformative elements, of this approach to teaching that seeks to let learning happen. Careful examination of the things said to be done and made in the course of instruction will help to clarify the fundamentally aesthetic principle that animates and informs the use of mnemonics, which in turn enables students to learn by reflecting on and building beyond what they think they already know.

# Chapter 2

## Letting Learning Happen

### I. Manifesto

My work is concerned primarily with questioning what animates the practical aspects of teaching and learning, aspects that precede any talk of standards, assessment or outcomes. Therefore I would begin this chapter with a sincere "call to thinking." I am building here on the startling pronouncement with which Martin Heidegger launched a series of lectures to his students on what is called thinking: "We come to know what it means to think when we ourselves try to think" (Heidegger, 1954/1968: 3).

Teaching, in this regard, is considered more difficult than learning, not because the teacher must have a larger store of information and have it always ready, but because "what teaching calls for is this: to let learn. The real teacher, in fact, lets nothing else be learned than—learning. . . . The teacher is ahead of his apprentices in this alone, that he has still far more to learn than they—he has to learn to let them learn" (Heidegger, 1954/1968: 15). Put more succinctly if cryptically: a teacher teaches most when not teaching. Indeed, this response points toward one way of understanding what I have in mind when I advocate that we strive to find ways of letting learning happen.

While any of a number of prominent typologies of learning could be used to discuss the challenge implicit in the charge "learn to let them learn," for the purposes of this chapter we will consider that learning: (1) is a lifelong process which arises from various conditions, (2) is experiential, (3) can not itself be observed, and (4) is cumulative (Jackson and Stoneback, 1997). As teachers, while we must bridge the gap between what the student knows and what the student is expected to learn, we cannot control all of the minutiae that go into someone "getting it," whether during a class session or an entire course of study. What we can do though is attend to the differences of the various types of learners we encounter. We can even study things like brain-wave feed-back to maximize optimum learning times, and we can follow the guidelines presented in detailed studies of this or that method designed to enhance instructional delivery and reception. And yet despite the most scientific approaches, and notwithstanding efforts to articulate instructional objectives as precisely as possible, and even taking into account the most sophisticated techniques for testing and measuring, still, we cannot ever really know exactly when and how a student has "gotten it"—speaking here, as above, more about fundamental concepts than about exact dates or data. For who can say or control what will get recalled, and subsequently translated into practical terms, from what once echoed in a large lecture hall?

For example a former student related to me that, once during an evening of hearty reveling with her peers she recalled and stood by something we had covered in class several semesters before—lines with which Raleigh answered Marlowe's shepherd urgently wooing a nymph: "If all the world and love were young, / And truth in every Shepherd's tongue, / These pretty pleasures might me move, / To live with thee, and by thy love." Mundane though this anecdote is, still we have a case in which literature helped someone make what in retrospect seems to have been a good choice regarding how to conduct and control herself at a decisive moment in her young life. Mundane or not, it confirms my belief that the seed of lifelong learning can take root only in the ground of human experience. For, as this anecdote indicates, whatever else may be said about it, at least learning of some sort, seemingly of its own and in its own time, happened. Had I not run into this student and had this chat though, I might not ever have known the extent to which, years before, I had been a conduit, with the help of Marlowe and Ralegh, to carry out what Heidegger argued teaching calls for: "to let learn."

The fundamental issue at stake here can be expressed in the form of a question, and one that warrants careful and sustained scrutiny: "Why doesn't more thinking and re-thinking occur in schools? Our position is that the mimetic approach to education is too compelling for many educators to give up. It is amenable to easily performed and widely accepted measurement, management, and accountability procedures. This approach has long dominated educational thinking, and therefore, policymaking" (Brooks and Brooks, 1993: 15-16). Rethinking (and that includes rethinking the very terms in which this proposition is cast) is fundamental to the educational reforms and adjustments discussed by Brooks and Brooks, and it is consonant with the forms of sound pedagogical reflection and committed social practices that I am suggesting we take to heart.

At the core of my assumptions about teaching and learning, the "nucleus of education," is that educational reform "must start with *how* students learn and *how* teachers teach, not with legislated outcomes" (Brooks and Brooks, 1993: 3-4). To start with the *hows* and not projected outcomes may seem to go against the stream of some developments in educational theory and practice today. When planning lessons, teachers almost always consider what information needs to be imparted so as to keep abreast of externally imposed demands; for example, course requirements, school-wide curriculum, state regulations, national mandates and funding qualification guidelines. Furthermore, teachers are bound to measure student learning against some approved (or at least accepted) standard. And yet what if, irrespective of the external forces, teachers focused their attention on the *hows* of teaching and learning? I would have us consider this further, for learning is not a neatly balanced equation with "outcomes" on the right-hand side of the equal sign and "method times curriculum" on the left.

The practical side of thought and action, which is desirable in the course of reflection *and* instruction, can be discussed in terms of process-oriented perspectives on learning (Schon, 1983). According to this model, what is termed "technical rationality" (associated with positivistic thinking and empirical observation) is separated from "reflection-in-action." And yet both modes of cognition, I maintain, still are grounded in the overarching conception made popular in America by John Dewey, that we know by doing. Neither of these methods of knowing (technical rationality on the one hand and reflection-in-action on the other) necessarily is better than the other; they are born of different conceptual frameworks (Slama, 1997). Situated with respect to one another, such conceptual frameworks (technical rationality and reflection-in-action) at times oppose one another and at times work in tandem to produce remarkable results. By the same token, educators frequently talk about "individual differences" among students, but, in actual practice, they tend to reward only the students who resemble themselves (Lindley, 1993: 27). What is more, students typically succeed whose thought processes tend to harmonize with those of the teacher and whose work products are consonant with the manner in which the lessons were delivered. And so, as only seems natural, we often adopt or develop grading mechanisms that reinforce our own favored ways of formulating and analyzing issues and problems—in short, ways that mirror and magnify our (often unconscious) biases of whatever sort. This gives us yet another good reason to hold "outcomes" within brackets for the time being and for us to focus instead on the *hows* of teaching and learning. Doing so, I am convinced, will provide us with a more encompassing and accommodating conceptual framework for thinking about, and thinking through (and for rethinking), educational reform whether in a particular classroom, across the curriculum, or even system-wide.

Careful reflection on the order that I am proposing here allows for different teaching styles purposefully to come into contact with and to overlap, and at key junctures to mesh with, various learning styles. Such on-going reflection-in-action can set the stage to let learning happen by allowing students to encounter what we would teach them first-hand. This is a practice at once grounded in and subsequently borne aloft by incisive questioning. More specifically, it is realized through engaging in the kind of questioning that needs to be learned; or, rather, that needs to be relearned, since it is often something we once knew how to do naturally and well but which, over time, became dissociated from our patterns of thought and action (Freire and Faundez, 1989: 35). This is the kind of questioning that tends to generate creative projects and original works of art in response to one's active engagement with the conceptual core of what one set out to study, explore, and learn. For this to happen regularly and authentically among one's students, a teacher must be willing, at timely intervals, to reflect purposefully on what he is doing (or thinks he is doing) when he says he is teaching.

This kind of rethinking, as I am discussing it here, can be thought of as part of the meta-cognitive component of one's teaching. It is integral to one's setting in play those practices that tend to be most conducive to letting learning happen. And this kind of rethinking needs to be a part of every student's self-conscious intellectual life as well. What I am describing then is a dynamic process, for teacher and student alike, that seeks (as Heidegger advocated as being the essence of what teaching calls for) to let learn.

By no means though is this a do-whatever-you-will approach to class-room activities. Indeed, as Heidegger went on to state explicitly, the teacher's job in such situations is pushed to the limit. It requires substan-tial focus on one's subject of instruction, sustained commitment to the highest goals of the profession, and the most rigorous kind of thinking about (and of rethinking) every aspect of what it is we would teach to others. This represents the hardest work a teacher can undertake—and it may well be the defining task of teaching.

Nowhere in this description of what I am calling dynamic teaching and learning have I used the term standards because this term, like out-comes, is charged with a host of culturally determined meanings that undermine the expansive kind of rethinking I am advocating we under-take each in our ways and each in our own time. Once such terms have been thoughtfully rethought from the ground up, with an eye toward learning how to let learn, then perhaps such terms once again can find an apt place in our discourse about the dynamic process of teaching and learning (and teaching *as* learning—learning to let learn).

# II. Demonstration

Recalling the mnemonic principles from the previous chapter, let us begin this section with a mind-map that encapsulates visually the main points to be explored in what follows [FIGURE 2.1]. It can be expressed as well, and in tandem, by a chart (or Memory Grid) [FIGURE 2.2]. The rest of this chapter then simply narrates the *hows* of a specific course of study. In the process, I am able to outline some of the key aspects of a conceptual framework, which offers a way to let learning happen. By reviewing the main assignments, syllabus, and goals of a course for secondary-school teachers that I facilitated as part of an NEH/Council for Basic Education Summer Seminar, I aim to present a description of practical thinking, making, and doing that you can use and modify, irre-spective of projected (or mandated) outcomes, so as to coincide with— and hopefully in an effort to help you think about expanding the reper-toire of—your own teaching and learning style no matter what side of the desk you happen to occupy at any given time. As you will read in the description of the course toward the end of this section, I was the desig-nated teacher-scholar of the group and sought to model the innovations I was advocating. Some of the key assignments and interventions, while

**Figure 2.1**

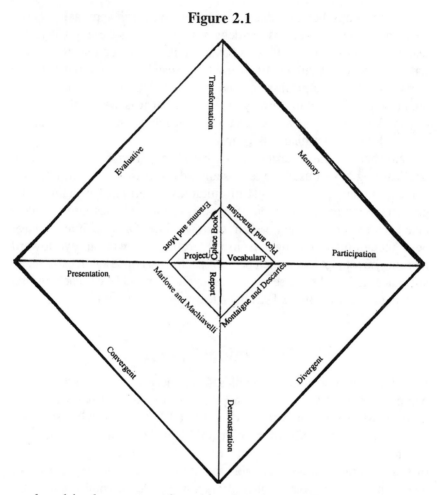

employed in the context of teaching Renaissance Humanism, are discussed in what follows so as to encourage you to contour them to fit your
own prospective needs.

First though, let me outline one of the main points that emerged
from my assessment of the teachers who were, in the context of the
seminar, my students. As the course unfolded, a fairly obvious point
came to my attention—one which took on greater significance as I came
to learn more about the backgrounds, objectives, and intentions of my
students (and thus was made to reflect more systematically on my own
motives and teaching methods). The point, which stands now as a recurring motif in my inquiry into what opens the way toward letting learning
happen is this: Just as learners tend to learn better according to one

Figure 2.2

## A SERIES OF USEFUL CORRESPONDENCES

| learning proclivity | TAXONOMIC | VISUAL | ASSOCIATIVE | META-CRTICIAL |
|---|---|---|---|---|
| type of question | MEMORY *What was it exactly?* | DIVERGENT *Why this and not that?* | CONVERGENT *How do these things relate?* | EVALUATIVE *What would happen if & how would I feel?* |
| mode of engagement | *PARTICIPATION* in the work by taking it on its own terms, as you find it | *DEMONSTRATION* of mastery of the material & ideas | *PRESENTATION* of the material in a way that speaks to you | *TRANSFORMATION* by bringing it home, and sending it back out into the world |
| assignment | VOCABULARY | REPORT | PROJECT | COMMONPLACE BOOK |
| authors | **Pico**, Paracelsus Mercator... | **Montaigne**, Descartes | **Marlowe**, Machiavelli | **Erasmus**, More |

approach over another, so too we teachers (no matter how hard we strive to switch up our methods of instruction or to shake up our delivery) tend to teach according to single style with which we have become comfortable and in which we place a great deal of confidence.

This may seem self-evident, but I maintain that there are times when the obvious needs to be stated; for, in its statement (or, more properly, its restatement), we can sometimes come to hear in it something that previously we took for granted. I do not mean here to invoke or to criticize any of the recent studies on the varieties of teaching styles or types of learners. Instead, in what follows, I want simply to point out and briefly discuss four appreciably different *learning proclivities* that emerged during the course of the seminar. They are taxonomic, visual, associative, and meta-critical [FIGURE 2.2, top line of the grid]. The last, meta-critical, is misspelled on the chart, and thus afforded an opportunity to discuss the self-reflective nature of this learning style—and to joke about why it might really bother someone devotedly taxonomic. These four general categories can, of course, be used to typify teaching styles as well. Further, each intellectual proclivity tends to be associated with certain kinds of questions that such a mode of learning generates (Guilford, 1959). Specifically, the taxonomic learner responds well to memory questions; the visual learner excels at those kinds of questions which are divergent from the main matter at hand; the associative learner likes to question how the given things being studied relate one to the other; the meta-critical thinker is prone to pose evaluative questions.

While there are other taxonomies of learning styles that could be cited here to explain or modify the grid which came out of my teaching that summer, there is much merit in considering the implications of this simple model while keeping in mind that it explains only the contours of each section so named. I am not claiming to offer a definitive map of learning types or teaching styles; neither am I claiming that the four corresponding classes of questions catch everything that can be thought in its net. Still, these questions do seem to coincide with what I happen to ask in my own classroom activities, and so—for me at least—they bear further elaboration, especially as they pertain to the useful correspondences I would bring to your attention in what follows.

The four types of questions (memory, divergent, convergent, and evaluative) have been explored by Daniel Lindley in terms of the "Craft of Teaching" as follows: "Memory questions reward students who find other sorts of questions threatening in one way or another. Convergent questions reward students with high intelligence—intelligence tests are convergent tasks. Divergent questions reward creative students but seem irrelevant and a waste of time to people whose preference is convergent thinking. Evaluative questions bring out the philosophers, the critics— the judgers" (Lindley, 1993: 20). While I would not advocate one kind of question over another in every instance, there are situations where one kind of question might yield more fitting responses than another kind given the trajectory of one's lesson, the nature of the material being studied, and, of course, taking into account projected outcomes. In saying this, I am acknowledging that (at least where questions are concerned), in practice, teachers tend to teach toward something. And yet I would return to Heidegger's timely warning that we "come to know what it means to think when we ourselves try to think." This applies as well to thinking about questions—and about the very nature of questions to presume some sort of answer. In this sense they have a lot in common with projected outcomes in the world of instructional objectives.

Once these four kinds of questions shaped themselves in my mind, the more I thought about them relative to the different types of learners I found myself teaching in the summer seminar. I discussed my findings with each of the students, and asked each to consider what I had identified about their learning in particular and how it might pertain to the notion of "letting learning happen" more generally. These discussions gave rise to the following paragraph, which I wrote up for my students in the hope that they might refer to it during the school year when once again they would be cast in the role of teacher:

*Which of these four kinds of questions do you tend to ask yourself when you are reading a text like one of the assigned books this summer? How does this compare to what you ask your students? You could bring this out, explicitly, in your teaching, if you like. If you do decide to do this though, may I suggest that you make sure you have your students keep in mind that a caper or question sheet of any kind (even, and especially, a test) reflects (and enables students to reflect on) pedagogical methods. With this in mind, you might instruct them as follows: "Ask yourself what kinds of questions (if any) your teachers ask you, whether on assignments or in class during discussions (or lectures). Ask yourself what sorts of questions you ask one another in study sessions, about non-academic things, about imponderables. To what extent does the way a question is formulated presume a certain kind of (if not a specific) answer? How can questions ever be more than merely rhetorical? Are there in fact certain sorts of questions to get at certain sorts of answers? What might they be? Would you want to begin your inquiry about questioning by analyzing the very questions posed here and perhaps reflect on the different ways they seek to stimulate thought— or do they foreclose the possibility of your asking other kinds of questions?"*

As it happened, I had constructed the course around four units, and there were four major kinds of exercises designed to enhance participation and which allowed the students to demonstrate each in their own way what they were learning. It ended up being the case that these four main types of assignments (vocabulary lists, reports to the class, independent projects, and commonplace books) each related to the four types of questions. Each of the four units was taught with this pattern in mind so that by the end of the term, with Erasmus (to follow along, down the right-hand side of the chart [FIGURE 2.2]), we were definitely in a meta-critical mode, relaying heavily on reflective thought, asking evaluative questions, and following the method perfected by Erasmus himself, the master of the commonplace book as a form of instruction and subsequent basis for lifelong learning. Our work in this, the last, part of the course tended to be Transformative—students sought to bring it all home and thence to send it back out into the world in some new form that they had created, each in their own way, so as to reflect not only what they had studied but also what they had learned.

The transformative aspect of the lessons, which was from the start an important part in my over all plan for the course, is not so easy to express as a single instructional objective involving *performance, conditions,* and *criterion* (Mager, 1975: 21). And yet it is for this reason that I have been compelled to find ways of making quite clear what counts. As a result, some of the final projects or "work products" (to use a term from political economics, and one to which I will return and analyze more thoroughly in Chapter 3) that have come out of my courses over the years have stood masterfully on their own as original works of art but which also reflected the range of research undertaken and the careful completion of all of the capers. Such new creations—for example, a one-act play which brought together Machiavelli, Montaigne, Henry VIII, and Martin Luther for a dinner party; a sculpture of the Renaissance Temple of Knowledge; or a lithograph at once mirroring and explaining the origins of European Print Culture—, each in its own way, demonstrated the student's control over a vast amount of information while transforming what she or he had learned into something truly original. Moreover, while the students drew on their own special skills and abilities, they all took supreme risks in the spirit of honest academic inquiry.

During the first week of instruction though, when students are trying to find their bearings, I have found it most appropriate to tend toward a more taxonomic approach. This helps the students figure out what, given the effluvium of seemingly undifferentiated information we encountered all at once, is going to be most useful to them, both individually and as a class, as the course proceeded. And so, as had been the case with my college courses, the teachers in this NEH summer seminar sought to engage and encounter the books first-hand, taking each on its own terms, reading them carefully and then, guided by capers, becoming more actively engaged with key aspects of each book. Specifically, since we were seeking to identify key elements of Renaissance humanism, we began by diving headlong into Pico della Mirandola's landmark declaration of intellectual independence (which in English is referred to as *On the Dignity of Man*). One student's map of the work reflected the taxonomic approach that is discussed and performed in this preamble to a debate written by Pico himself, the preeminent champion of early modern learning taxonomies [FIGURE 2.3]. Following the ideas of the author, Dialectic is shown to be the path leading into the Palace of Wisdom, the roof of which is supported by charity, justice, contemplation, moral philosophy, natural philosophy, and theology. This mnemonic mind map speaks volumes as it were, and serves as a viable itinerary (moving through the forest of pagan and Arabic learning) of the main points in this benchmark text in Western Thought.

And so in the next unit, beginning with Montaigne, even though we were not yet following the chart (which was just taking shape in my mind), we approached the assignment less taxonomically and more visually as the writing demanded. Moving to Descartes, we asked more divergent questions than before, consistent with his hyperbolic doubting of the way things were: "Why this and not that?" In the third unit, on Marlowe and Machiavelli, we thought more associatively than visually with respect to the questions asked and also in our realization of the assignments. This may have been due in part to the changing style of the capers that were given to the students at the beginning of each unit prior to their engaging the work of art under scrutiny; capers, as has been explained above, are imaginative study sheets designed "to let learn." I would point out also that capers can be designed to fit all manner of

## Figure 2.3

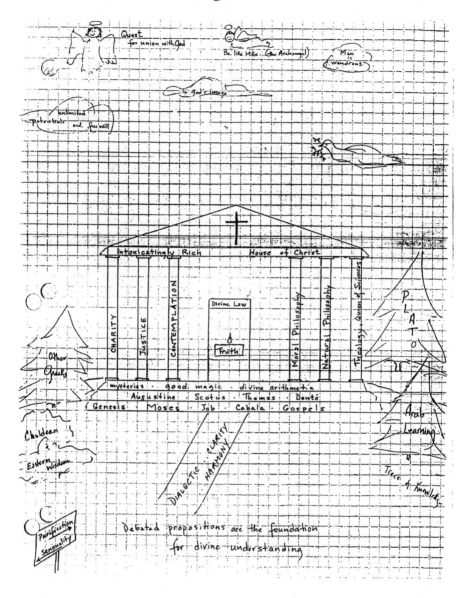

learners, no matter what stage they happen to be at in their education—or continuing education as will be discussed in greater detail in Chapter 4. Sometimes I make up capers for myself, especially when I am reading a book for the second or third time. This helps make me remain more attentive to image patterns, repeated verbs, and the field of favored adjectives so I can then make reasonable determinations about the world opened up through the author's art. (For example, I keep a list now of Kafka's repeated descriptions of windows in *The Trial* and in his reflections on suicide in his private correspondence; and a list of Virginia Woolf's intriguing and shifting images used to describe both water and the passing of time in *Mrs. Dalloway*.)

Taken together, the capers, along with the four kinds of assignments which included an individual report to the class (the next to the last line on the chart [see again FIGURE 2.2]), formed a kind of learning dynamic in their own right—and seemed to come out of the course expectations "at right angles," like the base of our pyramid [FIGURE 2.4].

**Figure 2.4**

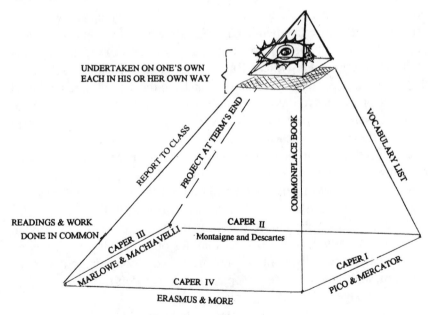

UNDERTAKEN ON ONE'S OWN
EACH IN HIS OR HER OWN WAY

REPORT TO CLASS

PROJECT AT TERM'S END

COMMONPLACE BOOK

VOCABULARY LIST

READINGS & WORK
DONE IN COMMON

CAPER II
Montaigne and Descartes

CAPER III
MARLOWE & MACHIAVELLI

CAPER IV
ERASMUS & MORE

CAPER I
PICO & MERCATOR

EACH INDIVIDUAL'S PYRAMID OF STUDIES, BY WHICH ONE MAKES A STEADY ASCENT OF KNOWLEDGE; AND CONDUCING TO THE LEAP TOWARD WISDOM

And once we made the leap from a flat two-dimension diagram [FIG-URE 2.1] to the idea of a three-dimensional one [FIGURE 2.4], we were better able to visual the dynamic aspect of what we were learning about and how we might rethink the ways in which we represented it. In making this leap, the students saw an analogy to the leap toward wisdom that we each would have to make on our own, in our own time and through whatever means and special talents were available to us. By the same token, this pointed the way toward leaping into other ways of conceptualizing the models we had been using to think about our work—and indeed, models (or conceptual frameworks) about thinking itself. In this sense we had found a way to think beyond the conceptual framework with and through which we had initiated our models for thinking about, and rethinking, Renaissance Humanism, the nominal theme of our course.

We were guided in this direction from the outset though by virtue of a motto given to the course of study ("Man is the measure of all things"); a motto, whose undergirding assumptions we sought steadily and continuously to rethink from the ground up with every new text or assignment encountered. One student, in his commonplace book, aptly depicted and described this very inquest by taking as his intellectual home-base da Vinci's rendering of Vitruvian Man, which shows divine proportion literally embodied in man. Situating his effort beneath a hand-printed heading of our course motto, Dr. Fuller worked ingeniously with a rendering of a typical Humanist response to earlier scholastic thought (in this case, the paradox of "squaring the circle") and applied it first to his reactions to Pico's treatise [FIGURE 2.5]. Then he went on to apply the same image, rewrought according to the themes uncovered in each of the other units [FIGURE 2.6]. Thus the top-left relates to Marlowe's thematization of modern man as heroic if doomed in his over-reaching by virtue of his own strength, an Icarus-type; the top-right continues this performative meditation on man's re-negotiated place in the cosmos, between angel and beast, as portrayed in Renaissance English drama; at the bottom-left, the segmented parts of the Vitruvian Man symbolically echo the painful realities of corporality as discussed by Montaigne, who lived and wrote during the bloody French Wars of Religion; and the bottom-right depicts Erasmus's deft transformation of the noble image of Renaissance man into a fool.

While many more such examples could be cited to indicate the ways that learning was allowed to happen and to suggest the extent to which, in the short run at least, the design of the course furthered a sincere call

# Figure 2.5

# HOMO EST MENSURA OMNIUM RERUM.

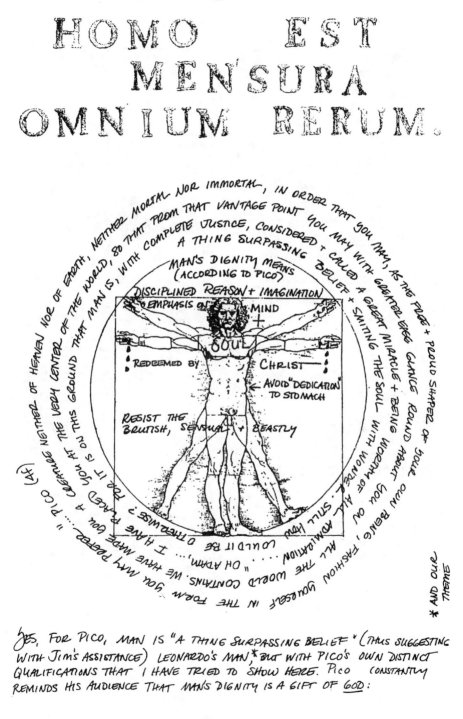

MAN'S DIGNITY MEANS
(ACCORDING TO PICO)

DISCIPLINED REASON + IMAGINATION
— EMPHASIS ON MIND

SOUL

REDEEMED BY          CHRIST

AVOID "DEDICATION"
TO STOMACH

RESIST THE
BRUTISH, SENSUAL + BEASTLY

"... NEITHER MORTAL NOR OF EARTH, NEITHER MORTAL NOR IMMORTAL, IN ORDER THAT YOU MAY, AS THE FREE + PROUD SHAPER OF YOUR OWN BEING, FASHION YOURSELF IN THE FORM YOU MAY PREFER. ... I HAVE PLACED YOU AT THE VERY CENTER OF THE WORLD, SO THAT FROM THAT VANTAGE POINT YOU MAY WITH COMPLETE JUSTICE, CONSIDERED + CALLED A GREAT MIRACLE + BEING WORTHY OF ALL ADMIRATION ... ALL THE WORLD CONTAINS. WE HAVE MADE YOU A CREATURE NEITHER OF HEAVEN NOR OF EARTH ... SO THAT YOU ON THIS GROUND THAT MAN IS, WITH COMPLETE JUSTICE, CONSIDERED + CALLED A THING SURPASSING BELIEF + SMITING THE SOUL WITH WONDER — STILL HOW COULD IT BE OTHERWISE? ... "OH ADAM," ... I HAVE MADE YOU ... TOO IT IS ... " PICO (AF)

* AND OUR THEME

YES, FOR PICO, MAN IS "A THING SURPASSING BELIEF" (THUS SUGGESTING WITH JIM'S ASSISTANCE) LEONARDO'S MAN,* BUT WITH PICO'S OWN DISTINCT QUALIFICATIONS THAT I HAVE TRIED TO SHOW HERE. PICO CONSTANTLY REMINDS HIS AUDIENCE THAT MAN'S DIGNITY IS A GIFT OF _GOD_:

# Figure 2.6

TILL SWOLN WITH CUNNING, OF A SELF-CONCEIT,
HIS WAXEN WINGS DID MOUNT ABOVE HIS REACH,
AND MELTING, HEAVENS CONSPIRED HIS OVERTHROW...

MARLOW, DR. FAUSTUS, pro. 2

SEE ACTS 8:9 (SIMON MAGUS, the SORCERER)

FROM Wm. SHAKESPEARE'S HAMLET:

WHAT A PIECE OF WORK IS A MAN, HOW NOBLE
IN REASON, HOW INFINITE IN FACULTIES, IN FORM
AND MOVING, HOW EXPRESS & ADMIRABLE IN ACTION,
HOW LIKE AN ANGEL IN APPREHENSION, HOW LIKE
A GOD! THE BEAUTY OF THE WORLD; THE PARAGON
OF ANIMALS; AND YET TO ME WHAT IS THIS QUINTESSENCE
OF DUST? (2.2. 302-308)

IF YOU STOP READING THIS QUOTE TOO EARLY, YOU LOSE THE
TENSION BETWEEN MAN AS A "GOD" + MAN AS "DUST."
CERTAINLY, THE PRAISE OF MAN'S REASON, FACULTIES, +
APPREHENSION COMPARE FAVORABLY WITH PICO. REMEMBERING
MAN'S MORALITY ("DUST") STRIKES ME AS MORE MARLOVIAN,
AND PERHAPS, AS HARRY LEVIN SUGGESTS, CHARACTERISTIC
OF DRAMA IN GENERAL (THEATER ITSELF BEING TEMPORAL +
OFTEN EMPHASIZING THE MORALITY OF ITS LARGER-THAN-LIFE
HEROES FOR DRAMATIC EFFECT).

WHAT A PIECE OF WORK IS A MAN...

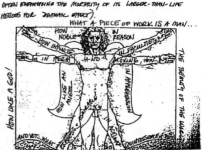

FROM MONTAIGNE'S ESSAYS ("ON CRUELTY"):

I COULD HARDLY BE CONVINCED UNTIL I SAW IT,
THAT THERE WERE SOULS SO MONSTROUS THAT THEY
WOULD COMMIT MURDER FOR THE MERE PLEASURE
OF IT; HACK + CUT OFF OTHER MEN'S
LIMBS; SHARPEN THEIR WITS TO INVENT
UNACCUSTOMED TORMENTS + NEW FORMS OF DEATH, W/O
ENMITY; W/O PROFIT, + FOR THE SOLE PURPOSE OF ENJOYING
THE PLEASING SPECTACLE OF THE PITIFUL GESTURES +
MOVEMENTS, THE LAMENTABLE GROANS + CRIES, OF A MAN
DYING IN ANGUISH. FOR THAT IS THE UTTERMOST POINT
THAT CRUELTY CAN ATTAIN. (315-316)

MOST ASSUREDLY, MONTAIGNE DOES NOT SHY AWAY FROM
WHAT HE CALLS MAN'S "NATURAL PROPENSITY TOWARD CRUELTY"
+ "INSTINCT FOR INHUMANITY (?)". WHILE PICO DOES SAY MAN HAS
A CHOICE WHICH FLOOR TO CHOOSE ON THE FREE WILL
ELEVATOR (FROM THE LOWER BRUTISH FLOORS TO THE UPPER

"GOOD WITS HAVE ALWAYS BEEN ALLOWED THE LIBERTY
TO EXERCISE THEIR HIGH SPIRITS ON THE COMMON
LIFE OF MEN, + W/O REBUKE, AS LONG AS
THEIR SPORT DOESN'T BECOME SAVAGERY...
IF SOMEONE ATTACKS THE VICES OF HUMAN
KIND ... IS HE HARMING PEOPLE
OR RATHER TEACHING THEM,
ADMONISHING THEM? CONSIDER
IN ADDITION ON HOW MANY
SCORES I ATTACK MY
OWN SELF. BESIDES, WHEN
MEN OF EVERY DIFFERENT
SORT ARE CONSIDERED, IT'S
CLEAR THAT VICE IN
GENERAL IS THE TARGET,
NOT A PARTICULAR
PERSON"
(ERASMUS, PREFACE TO FOLLY 5)

WHILE THIS IS MOST CLEARLY ERASMUS' DEFENSE OF
SATIRE, IT ALSO SAYS A GREAT DEAL ABOUT HOW
HE VIEWS HUMANKIND: PRONE TO VICE + IN
NEED OF "ADMONISHING" BUT ALSO CERTAINLY TEACHABLE, REDEEMABLE
IN THE SAME PREFACE (HIS LETTER TO T. MORE), ERASMUS PRAISES HIS OWN
"LEARNING" + "WIT" (3). BOTH ADAGES + THE COLLOQUIES
ALSO REVEAL ASPECTS OF HIS UNDERSTANDING OF HUMAN NATURE.
IN ADAGES, ERASMUS DISCUSSES THE OPPOSITE SAYINGS: HOMO
HOMINI DEUS + HOMO HOMINI LUPUS. ABOUT THE FIRST, ERASMUS

to thinking, let me turn now and reach for a conclusion. I do so by reproducing the document that gave the students their common point of departure, as well as an implicit contract, which allowed them to acknowledge the parameters of their commitment to the course of study. As such it can serve as a springboard for jumping off into other areas of study and for designing courses that involve disciplines other than those discussed here. And so, by the end of this section, it will become clear how such a "Plan of Study," combined with its designated "Motto, Expectations, and Key Questions," puts into action the main ideas presented so far in ways that can help you further your own instructional objectives and curricular goals.

## 1. Plan of Study

We plan to study Renaissance literature and intellectual history, especially as it pertains to the humanist motto "Man is the measure of all things." As teachers who work primarily in art, history, literature, and philosophy, we have come to realize just how much of what we do in the classroom has been shaped by the unprecedented flowering of classical learning and political thought during the Renaissance. We want to look more deeply into this remarkable period. Of the many works from which we might have chosen to make our reading list, we were concerned that our books all be "benchmark texts"—those books to and against which previous and contemporary works were compared (and continue to be compared). We also wanted to be reasonable in our expectations about what we could "master" during summer recess. To help us narrow the aperture further, we selected works, which, owing to their episodic structure, would lend themselves to practical classroom use in the years ahead. Also, because of our desire to build on our areas of interest and expertise, we chose books relating to literature and philosophy. Finally, in an effort to get the most out of the books selected, our scholar, Bill Engel, grouped them so they could be read in conjunction with and at times against one another. Each grouping includes two secondary-sources that address and illuminate key aspects of our course's main theme especially as it relates to a topic raised in that particular unit. The proposed outline of the four units, each with its own topic and region of focus, clarifies the trajectory of our seminar:

# 1st Unit:     Macrocosm & Microcosm     (focus on Italy)

We will begin by examining the humanist idea of "Renaissance Man" and his relation to the cosmos—whether seen through a telescope or microscope, a grid or a chart—using sketches by Leonardo da Vinci, images from Alberti's *On Painting*, maps by Mercator and Finé, excerpts from the pseudo-medical writings of Paracelsus, and Pico's *Oration on the Dignity of Man*. Secondary sources are Clark Hulse, *The Rule of Art: Literature and Painting in the Renaissance* (Chicago: University of Chicago Press, 1990) and Tom Conley, *The Self-made Map: Carto-graphic Writing in Early Modern France* (Minneapolis: University of Minnesota Press, 1996).

# 2nd Unit:     Discovery of the Self     (focus on France)

Montaigne's *Essays* and Descartes's *Discourse on Method* and *Meditations* enable us to question and reflect on the emerging relation that Renaissance Man (a term we will interrogate throughout our study) cultivated with himself—as an individual. Secondary sources will include Dawn Eng's translation of Friedrich's landmark study of Renaissance mental life *Montaigne* (Berkeley: University of California Press, 1991) and Dalia Judovitz's *Subjectivity and Representation in Descartes: The Origins of Modernity* (Cambridge, 1988).

# 3rd Unit:     The Will to Power     (focus on England)

Machiavelli's *The Prince* provides apt grounding for us to analyze the extremes of Renaissance Man's relation to his fellow men, especially as they are staged through Marlowe's *Doctor Faustus, Jew of Malta,* and *Tamberlaine, Parts I & II*. Secondary sources include Harry Levin's *The Overreacher* (Cambridge: Harvard University Press, 1952) and David Moore's translation of Federico Chabod's *Machiavelli and the Renaissance* (New York, 1960).

# 4th Unit:     World of Words     (focus on Holland)

The final unit will focus on the travels and travails and translations of an exemplary Renaissance Humanist, Erasmus of Rotterdam. We will read his *Praise of Folly,* most of the *Colloquies,* and selections from his collected *Adages*. Secondary sources will include Roland H. Bainton,

*Erasmus of Christendom* (New York, 1969); Erika Rummel, *Erasmus as a Translator of the Classics* (Toronto: University of Toronto Press, 1985); Michel Foucault, *Madness and Civilization* (New York, 1973).

## 2. Motto, Expectations, and Key Questions

*HOMO EST MENSURA OMNIUM RERUM.* One way of translating this maxim, which will guide our inquiry throughout the summer, is "Man is the measure of all things"—where the term "man" is understood to encompass all sentient, mortal beings. This theme has a long lineage; it has been and remains subjected to a variety of interpretations, from classical times (Protagorus, Pythagoras, and Aristotle), up through the Renaissance (Machiavelli, Montaigne, and Descartes), and well into our own day (Merleau-Ponty, Heidegger, and Derrida). Perhaps the most standard of the Renaissance understandings of this adage was summed up well in the writings of Paracelsus, and its most radical if polite critique came from Pico della Mirandola—both of whom we will read the first week. *HOMO EST MENSURA OMNIUM RERUM* became a kind of humanist by-word, and so we too will take this motto to heart even as we hold it up to rigorous scrutiny. We realize that a summer—or a decade of summers for that matter—cannot give us a full picture of the Renaissance. What we can do, though, is work closely with a series of exemplary texts that will give us access and viable in-roads to the political, religious, and intellectual commonplaces and complexities of the Age.

With this end in mind each of us will keep a running VOCABULARY LIST, which will serve as one of four corner-stones preparing a solid foundation for our building something useful and long-lasting out of what we will have learned in this summer seminar. All of the writers we are studying worked from COMMONPLACE BOOKS, and so we too shall keep them to record and gloss memorable quotations, sayings and deeds. CAPERS, spirited leaps of thought charted out on paper, will help us organize our notes and thoughts on the books for each unit. Group capers, in which Mind-Maps figure significantly, will come at the end of each unit meeting. Part of every Renaissance Humanist's training included copying out passages from the masters (often translating them from Latin) and then imitating their style. The point was to be able to compose extemporaneously a case for or against anything. One might praise a fly or write "A Complaint of Peace" (as did Erasmus). Therefore *IMITATIO* exercises will give us another way to show the extent to which we have become involved with the material, thought deeply about it, and sought to transform it in a style consistent with the principles informing the original and yet which is wholly our own work. Each *imitatio* will draw heavily from the reservoirs of our Commonplace Books, Vocabulary Lists, and Capers, and will include a critical introduction clarifying what we judge we have achieved (or fell short of achieving). All of these materials will be gathered together in a portfolio. Not only will this serve as an itinerary of our course of study, but also as the basis for our Spring Workshop when we will turn our attention toward transmuting them into the gold of practical classroom lesson plans. In the long run, by virtue of our having worked on and compiled our portfolios, we will be in a position to make a good case for certain curricular changes at our home institution.

The various writers we propose to study, each in his own way, was concerned with and was aware of the subjective complexities associated with "man" declaring himself to be the universal measuring stick. And who will measure the measurer? This last question (which can be answered readily if incompletely by the responses "God," "Death," or "One's Self") is what we will strive to locate in each of our authors. Additionally, we will pose the following questions (in ways appropriate to each author's chosen genre, topic, and project): by what authority does one presume to measure, and to create anew various standards of measurement? Measurement relative to what and to achieve what end? This line of questioning will enable us to "get inside the mind" of Renaissance Humanist writers while at the same time, by virtue of the secondary reading, maintaining a serious and responsible dialogue with the original works. Through our questioning we will reflect critically on the issues and texts so that we can weave them back into what we teach. We have put together readings and assignments that are designed to help us discover our own ways of questioning the tacit assumptions underlying the often-repeated sentence *HOMO EST MENSURA OMNIUM RERUM*. Each of the four units, with its respective variations on the theme, will help us recognize the motto's special implications in early modern literature, which we can then tease out and apply in our seminar presentations, group projects, and culminating in our commonplace books and course-portfolios. Like the Renaissance writers we are studying, our main objective is to integrate what we learn into our own lives—both within and outside the classroom. For, above all else, we are convinced that the works of literature we are studying have important things to tell us about how to live virtuously, and about how we can lead our lives more creatively and more deliberately.

* * * * *

Never again will such a course be taught, even if the same Plan of Study is used and even if the same students took (or taught) the course. Even if the material remains constant year after year, each course is unique—because of the particular students, the serendipity of the moment, each class, the social dynamics. . . . I selected this course though as a case in point because of its uniqueness and assuming that few if any would be in a position to say "that is just the sort of course I am planning to teach." But this in no way deters you from adapting the underlying aesthetic and mnemonic principles in delivering your courses and in imagining how otherwise to organize them with or without the latest developments in computer assisted learning. In fact the potentially alien nature of this course to your own disciplines or usual offerings, makes it all the more easy to see how it could provide a pattern capable of accommodating within it infinite variety—including your course content. For what I am interested in conveying here is a way of thinking about how you go about thinking about your teaching and learning, rather than to provide a template for how to actualize what you think you have to teach or learn. I offer an approach for you to learn "to let learn."

And so it is with this in mind that I would conclude this chapter with a Credo, couched in terms of encouragement to all of us who take to heart the implications and consequences of just such a call to thinking, one linked to an approach to teaching that seeks to let learn. It is appropriately titled insofar as a college student who attended one of my "Visiting Lectures" wrote on her exit-slip: "you remind me of my minister because you speak with such enthusiasm and passion on the topic"; and another, "you made me start to care." Credo literally means "I believe." As a literary form, a Credo records a set of beliefs, which clarifies where you stand, and thus how you intend to carry yourself in the world— especially as you relate to others.

# III. Credo

I believe that the purpose of teaching is to let learning happen. Sometimes this means just getting out of the way and keeping your opinions to yourself, and other times it means intervening in decisive ways to make clear to students your seasoned, critical judgments about the material being studied. I take Plutarch at his word that we are all capable of making progress in virtue and capable of detecting signs of our approach toward it.

> [I]t is our duty to compare our present emotions with their former selves and with one another, and thus determine differences. We must compare them with their former selves, to see whether the desires and fears and angry passions which we experience today are less intense than they used to be, inasmuch as we, by means of reason, are rapidly getting rid of the cause that kindles and inflames them; and we must compare them with one another, to see whether now we are more inclined to feel shame than fear, to be emulous rather than envious, more eager for good repute than for money (Plutarch, 1986: 445, 447).

I believe it is always preferable to be direct and honest with and about oneself. This is especially true for teachers. How else could we be trusted to work with those who have come to us in earnest that we might help them shape their ideas and earn their diplomas, and over whom we exercise some degree of authority whether in the form of grades or status or simply experience? And so, my Credo is simple—and it can be yours too, in part or in whole.

I believe that remarkable works from the world's great traditions can tell us useful things about how others have viewed and expressed what it means to be better, more ennobled, humans; and, further, that we stand to learn a great deal from those accounts. Whatever our areas of specialization, it is our task to go to the material we plan to teach—whether a differential equation, Javanese harmonics, toplogical functions, Qu'ran hermeneutics, the Periodic Table of Elements, the AIDS quilt project, Korean printmaking, political economic formulas, Dante's *Divine Comedy*, Buddhist monastic history, or van Gogh's "Bedroom at Arles." It is our further task to enter it, and to become a part of it. Then and only then can we allow it to become an abiding part of ourselves. It is in such moments of communion and transfiguration that, I believe, what we seek to teach comes alive and continues to live a renewed life in and through us. We give it life, even as it animates us.

I believe those who profess to be teachers must dedicate their lives to the pursuit of learning, and must think constantly and deeply about what it means to be a teacher. A teacher is someone who has made a deliberate decision to be dedicated to learning and then to share what she or he has learned—and continues to learn—while teaching. I have found a maxim that expresses this well: "cum docimus, discimus" [we learn as we teach]. Another motto by which I live and learn, closely related to the first, is "discere vivendo" [to learn through living].

I believe that, in addition to honoring our students, we have obligations to the books and concepts and axioms and facts that we teach as well as to the community within which we happen to be teaching and (it is to be hoped) learning. And yet, above all, I believe an educator should put his or her students first, and in this way contributes meaningfully to the Commonwealth of Learning. It is this that enables our lessons, over time, to circulate and reverberate honorably and amply in the communities of which our students are a part. This we do without any thought of personal advancement or private gain. There is no reward like no reward—as one teacher of old put it so eloquently if cryptically.

I believe a teacher is someone who makes an on-going effort to listen to what students are saying, to clue in to how they learn and to act on this appropriately. No matter what or how we teach, it becomes our responsibility to help students learn enough to be able to pose appropriately *prior questions*; namely, those fundamental questions upon which the very ground of what they think they know is based. This means that teachers have a nearly sacred trust and duty where their students are concerned. Bertrand Russell said it well in his essay on "Freedom Versus Authority in Education": "No one is fit to educate unless he feels each pupil an end in himself, with his own rights and his own personality, not merely a piece in a jig-saw puzzle, or a soldier in a regiment, or a citizen in a State. Reverence for human personality is the beginning of wisdom, in every social question, but above all in education" (Russell, 1977: 152).

I believe that no matter what class or what topic I might happen to be teaching, everything I do should be geared toward helping students see what they will be able to do with what they have been studying. Often for me this takes the form of having the students write critically or creatively (and often both at the same time) about what they have been studying, and at times to write in imitation of the book they have been reading (for example, to insert "three lost stanzas, newly recovered" in Edmund Spenser's *Faerie Queene*). But this is just a preliminary step. I believe further that every teacher is obliged to know in advance and to be able to state clearly what he or she wants the students to be able to do with the content of every lesson that is taught. It is in this respect that the real job of a teacher is to discover ways of helping students gain confidence and competence in learning how to learn what they need to know so that, along the way, they can begin to take a more active, reflective, and responsible role in their learning.

I believe the ultimate role of the teacher is to be there for one's students as they "get" a particular lesson or book, and then seek to move beyond the mere content of the instruction toward the more far-reaching implications and underlying principles. This is as true when I train fencers to riposte as it is when I show writers how to use the semi-colon. To be sure, the acquisition and mastery of basic skills proper to each discipline is vital to working effectively within that area of investigation. Still, once these basics are presented and "learned," I labor to help my students discover within themselves their own characteristic excellence; to discover for themselves how these basis skills can help them draw out, buttress, and build on their native abilities and intellectual preferences. I strive to enable them to recognize their strengths so as to cultivate them and then apply what they have learned to other areas of study and activities in the world. Sometimes this means taking the time to get to know how each of them learns. To do this honestly and with integrity a teacher must strive to respect the worth and dignity of every student—and often mark up a lot of homework assignments. Rather than subscribe to the doctrine of "student management" (which maintains that any time given to students is time away from your own, "more important," work), an educator must take seriously the charge implied in the etymology of the word education, *to lead*, (or, more accurately still, *to draw out*).

I believe it is our challenge and our reward, as educators, to lead our students out of and away from ignorance and toward a path most appropriate for their seeking a heart of wisdom and subsequently acting nobly in the world. The essence of my teaching, and what I hope to instill in each of my students (even as I strive to learn it anew each time I put it to the test), is summed up well by Montaigne in his essay "On Experience":

> To compose our character is our duty, not to compose books, and to win, not battles and provinces, but order and tranquillity in our conduct. Our great and glorious masterpiece is to live appropriately. All other things, ruling, hoarding, building are only little appendages and props, at most (Montaigne, III.13: 851f.).

# Chapter 3

---

# Speaking of Teaching

This chapter, appropriately placed at the center of the book, seeks simply to shine a little light on the ground of a problem. Specifically, I want to call attention to the predominantly verbal way we come to terms with art; and, by extension, with other closely related domains of inquiry and endeavor, like philosophy and like education. But I would issue a warning: this chapter, more so than the others, is extraordinarily careful in its precise use of words. Also, by the self-conscious use of repetition, this chapter seeks to turn the tables on a dominant—and predominating—view of pragmatic aesthetics that (1) focuses on products and measurable outcomes to validate and verify artistic activity, and (2) is superficial in its conception of truth as being essentially causal, consequential, and mimetic. Alternatively, this chapter insists, albeit in a way that seeks intentionally to short-circuit traditional discursive strategies, that (1) process needs to be balanced into the equation of assessing the value of work, and (2) truth gets concealed in the folds of fair approximations and faithful representations of what is held up as being the standard, which, we are told by experts and public opinion alike, we should be seeking to follow, reproduce, and imitate.

Repetition, unlike imitation, can help us see things, like ideas, in several ways at once—especially things we think we already know. As was discussed in Chapter 1, this was the principle underlying my assigning the same caper at different times during the semester and thus, it was hoped, at different stages of the student's itinerary of learning. Let us loop back further still to the Introduction, and consider in a new light the

passage quoted in connection with my insistence that whatever and however we may try to think, we think within the tradition.

> The assumption of the tradition is *not* necessarily traditionalism and
> the adoption of prejudices. The *genuine repetition* of a traditional ques-
> tion lets its external character as a tradition fade away and pulls back
> from the prejudices. . . . Thus, the contact with the tradition, the
> return to history, can have a double sense. On the one hand, it can be
> purely a matter of traditionalism, in which what is assumed is itself not
> subjected to criticism. On the other hand, however, the return can also
> be performed so that it goes back *prior* to the questions which were
> posed in history, and the questions raised by the past are once again
> originally appropriated (Heidegger, 1992: 138).

In the critique that follows, I too am working from within, even
while striving to twist free from, the sphere containing and conceptualized in terms of the tradition. I want to show how the words we use to
express arts related activities, no less than our educational goals, determine (and, in effect, predestine) what we end up discovering time and
again in our students' work, and thus what we end up teaching. I will be
taking as my point of departure the visual arts, although it takes no great
conceptual leap to see how what I am uncovering about the visual arts
applies as well the performing arts—including, perhaps the most
performative of all arts, teaching. Also I would alert you from the outset
that the words "conceptual" and "leap" are not used haphazardly here;
far from it, these terms will be subjected to critical scrutiny as this chapter proceeds and used at key junctures when my argument begins to
signal that it is about to take another turn.

By having us reflect critically and carefully on small things like
these words and small things like what a second-grader ends up making
in an art class, I believe we can become more alert to the larger scope of
our actions as teachers who care about more than what we are merely
teaching. My goal, more specifically still, is to call attention to the power
that words can have over our actions to affect change in and through
education, whether for good or for ill.

\* \* \* \* \*

Once while passing through an elementary school hallway, I over-
heard an exchange that stayed with me: *"Today you have Art?"*— *"We go
to Art today."*

In what context can we imagine this being said? Certainly first in the innocuous way it was originally meant: regarding a class, an activity, a special event. But it also implied something more: an endeavor. What if an accomplished artist like Louise Nevelson, or an influential philosopher like John Dewey, and not a second-grader, had uttered those words? What meanings would then accrue? This is no mere exercise in analyzing speech acts, for the stakes remain high no matter the status of the speaker. Six-year olds, no less than women and men of accomplished skill and learning, are valid disclosers of the truth that art allows to happen in the world. But so are ten-year olds and thirty-year olds; and so why is it that agents of the school systems all but cease rewarding students for creating works of art after they leave elementary school? Why is art so quickly coded as being mere decoration, or made the province of what a handful of gifted draftsmen can do because of their innate abilities to represent recognizable things? I will pass over these and other conceptions of the place of art and artists in schools and in contemporary society, and will observe several things that I will flesh out further in what follows: There is something about art and aesthetic experience, that is at once enduring and ephemeral, that at once marks a trace of something that someone left behind and also projects what remains to be done next; there is something about the truth of art and the authentic aesthetic experience that pays no heed to age or schooling or background. This is not to say that art is universally recognizable as such. After all six-year olds, no less than women and men of accomplished skill and learning, are valid disclosers of the truth that art allows to happen.

Therefore, it is vitally important that we, as educators, learn to listen more carefully to what else is being said a sentence like "*We go to Art*"; and, in doing so, let us consider that: "Erudition about the form does not guarantee a knowledge of the words. . . . We must hear the literally taken word in such a way that we heed its directives in their pointing to the dictum. In such heeding we then hearken to what the word is trying to say. We exercise attentiveness. We begin to think" (Heidegger, 1994: 15). What better word to launch our effort to begin thinking than "art"? Through art let us begin to exercise our attentiveness.

* * * * *

"*Today you have Art?*" In this question let us hear the genitive aspect implied in the infinitive form of the verb: "to have." In this case:

Art pertains to one's character; it is something one can have; it is part of oneself, perhaps even it is integral to one's life, to human-life, indeed to humanity, itself. In the answer *"We go to Art today,"* let us also be attentive to the dative aspect implied in the infinitive form of the verb "to go." In this case: Art is understood not only to take place somewhere (on a table, in a basement, at a studio), a place where someone can go, but also it is understood as that which can be approached, as that which one approaches. In this going to Art, we hear the rustle of movement; a relationship, something one can enter and be a part of, and, in time, perhaps, something within which one can come to dwell. In such a dwelling some, for a time, can come to find shelter. Through such dwelling, not only is *thought* preserved, but also, in so doing, truth is sustained. Going to art, in preserving thought, sustains truth. In and through one's going to art, truth is sustained. Put more directly and less subjectively: Going to art sustains truth.

*"We go to Art today."*

In returning to the elementary answer to the question of whether one has art, we return to the direct and superficial sense of the sentence which establishes a fact regarding a place at a designated time: *"We go to Art today."* But after one has gone to "Art," and after whatever has taken place there subsequently has become part of one's experience, someone might well then ask: *"What did you do in Art today?"* Or to inflect it passively: *"What, in Art, was done?"*

Answers might include, depending on the medium used or lesson attempted or core-curriculum assignment assayed, answers might include: painting, drawing, sketching, sculpting, or any of a number of verbs of doing and making that imply creating. To what end? To what end is such art done and spoken of as having been done? To what end do we do art? To what end is art done? Can art truly be said to be done? In "done," the past tense of the verb "to do," I would urge us to attend to the deeper resonance of "pastness," for it speaks beyond the simple implications that have come to reside in the idiom "I am done," used for example to indicate that you have completed an assignment, like home-work problems or your grading for the term. Something else is happening in this saying of done. What else, beyond pastness, happens?

What can happen, and what a teacher of art or philosophy or literature, can let happen—I propose—is nothing less than the coming to presence of truth (which may or may not have anything to do with learning). When one does art so that truth is allowed to happen, what is it, really, that one is doing, or has done? Let us think about this, and dwell on it, and allow ourselves to build on this idea that the doing of art—when art can be said to be happening—opens up a world in which the truth of the work of art shines forth. In this shining, truth happens.

Before proceeding though I should clarify that the term "the work of art" can be used in several senses, and I would urge you to hear in the phrase, each time I use it in this chapter, more than one meaning. The work of art, used as a noun, implies a finished product; something that has been done and can be shown on its own—namely, an artwork. If art is seen as the subject of the phrase though, then the work of art connotes something else; something that is furthered or brought into being by virtue of art; that which art does. Art, of course, cannot make or do anything on its own; it requires an agent (as do many artists, especially those who have no head for business), and often it involves, though not always, an audience—whether real or imagined. Art works through us, even as we use art to work things out.

As must be clear by this point I am concerned in this chapter with attending to, and working with, language (even though language is that with which and on which I am working). My focus in this chapter concerns the power of words to shape what we do—especially when we are involved with art, when we engage art, and even when we are engaged in the *doing* of art, in *making* art. And so if my language at times in this chapter does not sound like ordinary speech or like the voice you heard in the earlier chapters, it is because I am trying to circle back and get inside of commonplace terms, so as to hear in them what they have all but ceased to disclose precisely because they are so much a part of everyday speech. If I have been extremely careful in my choice of words, it is because I am concerned, in general, with the path of language. To put it more emphatically: I am concerned with the way words tend to give us a *destination*, the way they can be said to *predestine* what we subsequently come to ask about and to know. More particularly still: I am interested in the extent to which words can predetermine what we end up finding in and through art (or philosophy or literary criticism or pedagogical theory) insofar as they set before us a course or track or path—for it is along just such a way, cut through the everyday, that art happens.

The image of a way or path is a common enough figure of speech; and, in a most telling way, it is taken up and followed by both Martin Heidegger and John Dewey in their discussions of the end of art. For both of them, "end" is understood more as a goal or projected aim rather than as a curt terminus. Although, to be sure, that sense must be heard in their use of the term as well, because, after all, it is firmly entrenched within Western cultural history. For example it is voiced in some circles as a lament ("there is no real art being made anywhere today"); in others as a celebration of overcoming what has, aesthetically speaking, been overcome ("the break from traditional, representational art has freed the artist to . . ."); and within the circle of continental philosophy, the idea of the end of art is being voiced as a vital, if conspicuously absent, part of the on-going discourse of metaphysics ("art, as conceived by the Enlightenment, is no more").

But to return to the metaphor as used by Heidegger and Dewey; the former wonders about the *way* of art. Way in German is translated *Weg*, which, as a noun also can mean path, route, road, walk, or errand; and, as an adverb (and this will take on greater significance in the conclusion to this chapter) means away, gone, and lost. Heidegger wonders: "in what way does truth happen in the work-being of the work?" (Heidegger, 1935-1936/1971: 50); while Dewey seeks to describe the indeterminate "path the work of art pursues" (Dewey, 1934/1980: 133). Although their writings on "the way" of the work of art, concerning the path taken toward authentic aesthetic experience in the world, appear at roughly the same time, neither sought to engage the findings of the other. Despite this, and notwithstanding the ever-widening ideological and political rift between Germany and America in the 1930's, their influential conclusions about the power of art and education to affect lasting social change are remarkably similar. Their determinations regarding the path pursued by the work of art might be stated: the aesthetic experience *can be said* to open up onto a world of truth.

The truth thus disclosed by the work of art, and the way it can be said to come to shine as a result, both happen to have been sketched out by Heidegger and also by Dewey, though each did so for reasons that are deeply imbedded in the course of his own lifework—and each did so in his own characteristic way and words. After all, philosophy, like educational theory, depends on discursive strategies to give coherence to aesthetic experience as well as other predominantly non-verbal activities. And yet, traditionally, we have come to rest easily with this mismatch of ways and means, of using words to characterize and disclose the truth of non-verbal experience and events. As ours is a culture that values visible marks, signs, tokens, and symbols, it is no wonder that words have been given pride of place. Heidegger and Dewey though, each in his own way, sought to confront, if not overcome, the difficulty presented by this immemorial state of affairs, by taking into account the texture and history of language in the process of expressing his ideas. For, like any medium, words have a materiality that is undeniable. It is a materiality, though, that sticks out into the world like a beam of light whose source is concealed, for what we can see is but a part of what gives rise to that which lets philosophy, like art, happen; and, in happening, happen as, and in terms of, shining truth. Such is the relationship between the medium and what it bodies forth when art happens. The materiality of language comes to our attention most often in the form of acoustic events or as graphic signs. But, by virtue of the way words never quite lose a trace of their non-material status, they tend to take on another, in some ways more authentic, dimension of reality—thus we can speak truthfully when we speak proverbially of being able to see past the surface to glimpse the immensity, perhaps even the extent, of an iceberg.

Words, one can argue, shape how we conceptualize, and subsequently come to engage, art. Words affect us: our feelings, attitudes, and choices. They affect how we come to know things, and how we make our way in the world. And, ultimately, then, words affect how we *do* things...things like art, like philosophy, like cultural theory, like teaching. *"What did you do in Art today?"*

In returning to, and repeating, this version of our question, let us hear in it something that has come to abide there. Let us hear something that we can dwell on, and, in time, come to dwell within—as a place of refuge, where things get preserved, things like truth; where art can be said to happen. Let us listen to what is carried on along within that phrase, for we stand to learn a great deal about how we consider art by reflecting on how we speak of art. First though, we need to attend to how, as children, we are taught and made to speak of art (and literature, and later philosophy), which often begins innocently enough by repeating what we hear. And there are rewards for this mimicry and punishments for falling behind in doing what is expected. But in time, even though we may take issue with this or that tenant and revise it a bit here and a bit there, the socially sanctioned discourse has already become so much a part of our speaking and indeed our thinking, that we cannot help but repeat and reproduce it. Necessarily it shapes and characterizes how we come to art, and come to do things through, or with, or to, art (or philosophy, or literary theory)—"the tradition."

*"What did you <u>do</u> in Art today?"* As stated—and thus as conceived— the question, as posed, presumes a process and, potentially, a product that resulted from the activity (as was discussed in the second section of Chapter 2). Therefore in the "do" let us relocate an implied "make." The basic assumptions remain the same: *"What did you <u>make</u> in Art today?"* Doing collapses into making. Of the many ways we might go about construing this, I will posit (in the next paragraph) three basic senses regarding the doing of art, regarding the making that makes "making art" a thing that one does and then is done with doing. Again my precise, if recursive, use of language is not intended as an exercise in semantics. I have adopted this way of setting up words, hyper-attentive to syntax, to provide a way to rethink the terms, especially the verbs, we use in speaking of art so as to get at what we are really doing when we say we are speaking of it (or of philosophy, and, by extension, of education). *"What was made in Art?"* By returning to, and turning about, the initial terms of the question in this way, we can glimpse shades of difference and meaning. We do so as if by accident, through the repetition— genuine repetition. This is a visual strategy appreciated fully and applied amply by, among others, Andy Warhol with his multiple Marilyns and Maos, his soup cans and soap boxes. (This would be a good place to include some figures to illustrate my point, but I have decided that, in the spirit of my approach to art through language, there can be no pictures in this chapter. I would invite you instead to imagine the examples just mentioned, whether from your own experience, or from what I am telling you about them, or from some combination of the two; or, not at all—if the last possibility is possible at all). *"What was done in Art today?"* Something was done. Something was made. *"What was made in Art?"*

The three main senses provisionally describing, and thus illustrating, the doing of art can be conceptualized as having various *charges*— like the old model that was used to explain atoms. First, the positive charge, which in the doing of art corresponds to putting something where nothing previously was. Second, neutrally charged: in making art corresponding to altering, arranging, connecting things ready at hand. And third, the negatively charged particle, corresponding to taking away something that previously was there. In that atomic model of "the building blocks of life," each type of charged particle was thought to keep the others in check.

In the first sense, the positive, we have verbs like those mentioned already, those considered the most elementary: painting, drawing, sketching. The second sense, the neutral, involves shifting, composing, or constructing; verbs like pasting, welding, tying, twisting, weaving, gluing. The last sense, the negative, calls on verbs like cutting, chiseling, sculpting, erasing, burning, dynamiting. . . . All three—whether adding, shifting, or subtracting—imply doing things to or through a particular medium. And all three might well come into play when it comes to the work of art opening up a world of truth, of possibilities. All three might well be preconditions for aesthetic experience. The truth of the work of art is disclosed through all three modes of engagement with the process of making or doing art; as such they can be said to be what lets art come forth, as shining truth. Recourse to all three modes of engagement in the making of art, can be seen in the light of what was said in the Introduction about the relation between order and chaos in teaching: Learning can happen even when we are not seeking to put something where we presume nothing previously was.

The verbs commonly used to describe activities relating to teaching, no less than those relating to art, do not pay proper tribute to the conceptual work involved. They tend to favor the activity part of the endeavor on the way toward realizing what you get in the end. Although the verbs primarily are process terms, ostensibly describing what was done, they tend to dwell on what someone in general did to make something in particular. The artist (the subject of this sentence which already is in motion and is well on its way toward a predetermined end) somehow acts on some material (verbs are words of action, even if that action is passive) to create something (the object, the product, the end). The process does not stop here though, since it is determined by the status of the product. What ends up getting made, the artwork, becomes something to which others (and the artist is included among these others) then can react. But where in all this activity are verbs like "imagine" or "design," verbs bespeaking the contemplation and planning that is fundamental to the doing of art? This was a point not lost on Dewey: "It is significant that the word 'design' has a double meaning. It signifies purpose and it signifies arrangement, mode of composition. . . . The characteristic of artistic design is the intimacy of the relations that hold the parts together" (Dewey, 1934/1980: 116-17).

Traditionally, it is the "idea" that mediates (it does not precede) "form" and "content." Here we can imagine, as has historically been the case, a split between art and craft, between art for art's sake (say, a collage or painting or wire sculpture) and the creation of something manifestly "useful" (say, a belt, a jug, a blanket) though it need not actually be used. It was Immanuel Kant who gave us what was to become the standard treatment of this theme in the West (Kant, 1790/1987: 171, §43). Dewey in turn gave a decidedly modern spin to the traditional Kantian formulation of the split when he wrote:

> Objects of industrial arts have form—that adapted to their special uses. These objects take on esthetic form, whether they are rugs, urns, or baskets, when the material is so arranged and adapted that it serves immediately the enrichment of the immediate experience of the one whose attentive perception is directed to it. No material can be adapted to an end, be it that of use as spoon or carpet, until raw material has undergone a change that shapes the parts and that arranges these parts *with reference to* one another with a view to the purpose of the whole. When this form is liberated from limitation to a specialized end and serves also the purposes of an immediate and vital experience, the form is esthetic and not merely useful [my emphasis] (Dewey, 1934/ 1980: 116).

Heidegger was likewise alert to the way works were potentially aesthetic. In his early work he argued that there is no such thing really as *a* useful thing (understood in terms of "something in order to," which is comparable to Dewey's "with reference to"). He argued that since there were different kinds of "in order to," such as serviceability, helpfulness, usability, and handiness, they constituted a totality of useful things. As the structure of "in order to" always contains a *reference* of something to something, he concluded that these things never show themselves initially by themselves. "A totality of useful things is always already discovered *before* the individual useful thing" (Heidegger, 1926/1996: 64). Words too were included among useful things, for words—as both a medium of communication and a means to do and make things (like points in philosophy)—also tell us what we have been thinking over time, including such an understanding of a traditional mode of making:

> We think of creation as a bringing forth. But the making of equipment, too, is a bringing forth. Handicraft—a remarkable play of language— does not, to be sure, create works, not even when we contrast, as we must, the handmade with the factory product. . . . [The Greeks] use

the same word *techne* for craft and art and call the craftsman and the
artist by the same name: *technites*. . . . However usual and convincing
the reference may be to the Greek practice of naming craft and art by
the same name, *techne* . . . signifies neither craft nor art, and not at all
the technical in our present-day sense; it never means a kind of practical performance. The word *techne* denotes rather a mode of knowing
(Heidegger, 1935-1936/1971: 58-59).

Irrespective of the relative validity of what the Greeks may or may
not have meant by the word, contemporary assumptions about the split
between *ars* and *techne* (based on medieval uses of the terms which
persist well into our own day) rest on the difference between divine
mystery and menial skill. On the one hand, a gift from the gods or a
natural ability; and, on the other, the concerted learning of a process that
enables one to *manu*facture something (recalling Heidegger's allusion to
the etymology of "handicraft," springing from the Latin for "hand"
[*manus*]). Of course there are seemingly infinite degrees of difference
between the poles of art and craft thus defined. For example, an accomplished craftsman is indeed an artist, and some artists are but tradesmen;
just as Nietzsche insisted on a distinction between academic laborers and
philosophers—the latter role which he claimed for himself only after
resigning his university post. But still these distinctions preserve in our
language, like flies in amber, something quite telling about our culture
regarding the status of doing and making. Significantly though these are
not the verbs that we would consider auxiliary, as being "helping verbs"
which make possible the construction of compound tenses (building on
verbs like "to have" and "to be"; as in, for example: "I have been
meaning to make sense").

A subject does something and then something is created. Heidegger,
too, will want to insist upon a distinction between "being created and
creation" and "making and being made" (Heidegger, 1935-1936/1971:
57). Creation, as discussed here, covers the extent of the three "charged"
senses outlined above; and yet creation need not be conceived of as
being generative: one can create by breaking, removing, or obliterating
something. Even "adding as creation" can be "destructive," for example
in Duchamp's mustachioed *Mona Lisa* we find a supplement that is a
kind of crossing out of, and thereby calls forth a reevaluation of, the
original, and thus calls forth a new, composite meaning. This fits the
definition of, but may not be exactly, what Dewey had in mind when he

referred to "the esthetic experience" as just such a path that the work of art pursues toward its coming into being, along which path "it keeps alive the power to experience the common world in its fullness. It does so by reducing the raw materials of that experience to matter ordered through form" (Dewey, 1934/1980: 133).

It was Nietzsche who ironically derived from within the tradition of philosophical inquiry the view that we create what is greatest by crossing out what has been—and this includes philosophy, and all that accompanies the highest achievements of Western rationalism. Both Dewey and Heidegger are writing in the shadow cast by Nietzsche's Zarathustra, though each may interpret his preferred brand of overcoming in different ways. Both, however, see the necessity of our embracing the power and will to affect changes in how we go about learning what we need to learn next. For as Dewey would have known, and as Heidegger studied intently, Nietzsche made us aware, through the words and character of his Zarathustra, our true humanity begins when we recognize the creative and productive power of negation and destruction. This is a concept that translates powerfully into authentic approaches to teaching geared to let learning happen, and also (as will be explored more fully in what follows) into the true work of art—into the *way* of art as self-overcoming.

> *I teach you the overman.* Man is something that shall be overcome. What have you done to overcome him? All beings so far have created something beyond themselves. . . . For must there not be that *over* which one dances and dances away? . . . There it was too that I picked up the word "over-man" by the way, and that man is something that must be overcome—that man is a bridge and no end. . . . I taught them to work on the future and to redeem with their creation all that *has been.* To redeem what is past in man and to re-create all "it was" until the will says, "Thus I willed it! Thus I shall will it!" (Nietzsche, 1884/1978: 12, 196-97).

To illustrate this as applies to the end of art (where end implies both a goal or aim, and also a terminal moment, or at least turning point, in the history of art), I would invoke the case of Rauchenberg's 1953 *Erased de Kooning Drawing*. Rauschenberg requested that de Kooning give him one of his most cherished drawings. Once he had it, he spent two months trying to eliminate the traces of de Kooning's original marks (Betti and Sale, 1980: 163). The result was a work of art, but can it be said, properly speaking, to be a new creation? Rauschenberg brought something into the world of art that had not previously been there. Can we say that something was made insofar the process was one of meticulously unmaking? Erasers have long been considered tools of the trade for draftsmen and for any artist using watercolor pencils, graphite, or charcoal; indispensable for shading and shadows. But still, was something done, or was something undone, in this endeavor? What was made or done; unmade or undone—or was it all of these at once?

Would the truth of art disclosed by Rauschenberg's endeavor be any less diminished if a six-year old erased pencil marks made by a peer—or a line drawing by Reubens? The world probably would never know about the former, though it would undoubtedly hear about the latter, which would be deemed scandalous since it took out of circulation something never again to be rendered by the master's hand (or that of his workshop). Rauschenberg's notoriety, and the public display of what *he* had done is what makes the general concept into an event in the history of art never again to be repeated with the same force. Though, to be sure, one can repeat this stunt over and over again to understand the mechanics of the exercise; but to do so would not to be furthering the trajectory of the arrow of the concept of the work of art toward its own overcoming. The same applies to educational methods: year in and year out the same sorts of exercises can be assigned to every student to impart specific target skills, and yet there are other, more vivid, approaches that could be attempted so as to leap beyond the confines of routine, imitative learning. Mere imitation preserves a superficial understanding of the truth of whatever is being learned or made, whether a five-paragraph essay or a work of art. Imitation can be the basis for future learning, but only if it is undertaken with the understanding that it is done *to be overcome*—that it is done so that it might be transformed into something more, into something beyond what it already is and otherwise is destined merely to be.

What keeps most people from such attempts, if not habit and satisfaction with the way things are, is the fear of not succeeding. The price paid however for the security and safety that comes from not doing anything to draw attention to or criticism about one's work is foregoing a potential leap—and in that leap, overcoming the tradition and traditionalism. The verbs used to describe how we respond to the work of art can be seen to apply as well to students' school work (whether writing spelling words in sentences, or one's conduct in the hallways) as to our peers' professional work (whether journal articles, or how well she discharges her administrative duties); verbs, like assessing, criticizing, admiring, approving, rejecting—in a word, *judging*.

So too the painter steps back from her canvas and the dancer may watch himself on videotape, the better to judge what should come next, to determine what needs to be undone, done differently, and touched up. What grounds such judgments? Obviously, as Dewey indicates, previous experience and the degree of one's training and professional expertise. But what else? What underlies our recourse to, recognition of, and knowledge about those previous experiences? Such judgments to a large extent are conditioned and determined by relative skill level. They are qualified by the parameters of an artist's conceptual project and by the judge's relative degree of expertise in that field of endeavor. And since judgments cannot help but be made, even by those who may not have the time or inclination to learn how best to assess what he is being called on to evaluate, often they are predominantly subjective—or, more often still, dependent on what the judge takes to be public opinion or the prevailing conception of standards then in vogue. And this brings us but a short step away from "taste" as being the final arbiter (with which there can be no disputing). The next step is a declaration of standards that legislates what "should be known" in the world of education, and what "should be made" in the world of art. In either realm the terms used to assess those on either side of the divide (good students as opposed to bad ones; good art as opposed to bad art) are supercharged with moral determinants, and imbued with standards reflecting often traditionally derived views of what is "in line" or "out of line," with what is within acceptable norms and what is not. It is an accepted tenant of the physical sciences, Heisenberg's Uncertainty Principle, that the act of measurement influences the phenomenon being measured. How tests are constructed, and what they are designed to test, invariably will affect the resulting evaluation, whether a critique of an apprentice's proposal or a student's final exam. Tests and grades do not just happen: we create them. Insofar as they are our creations, we alone are capable of overcoming them.

The step taken toward declaring standards of what others should be doing is a characteristically human thing to do. That step toward positivism (and away from overcoming) is part of the built-in survival instinct. Such tendencies may well be encoded in our DNA and thus are natural to us. If this is the case, and if turning this set of positive values on its head can be shown to produce a laudable end product, then, even by the terms of the tradition, it becomes the task of philosophy to educate us—to train us away from what is merely natural toward a higher kind of rational, sensible, and ethical way of living. Natural urges most often are what the educating environment seeks to tame and to sublimate (stay in line, raise your hand when you want to speak, no more than two boys to the bathroom at a time, no firearms on school grounds).

Rough behavior befitting the outlands is identified and modified, and then channeled and redirected into acceptable expressions of those instincts—or else the "un-teachable" student is disciplined and made part of someone else's workload. So much for schooling; education, on the other hand, has to do with transforming students into something more than they were, and helping them realize what more they can be; what they might become. The task of philosophy then is very much akin to, and perhaps overlaps with, that of education as it was outlined in the "Credo" at the end of in Chapter 2: to draw us out and away from ignorance. It becomes the task of philosophy to lead us *away from* such natural tendencies (understood here as being damaging to society no less than the spirit) to imitate and repeat—and thereby to make our own—judgments about what others should know, based on superficial understandings of truth that have been enshrined as standards. It is therefore the task of philosophy to *lead us toward* reflective thought and aesthetic action that pushes us beyond mere survival orientation and ultimately toward overcoming what is natural (and naturally harmful) to ourselves.

Thus continues, in a new guise, the age-old rift between art and nature. To what extent though, if at all, does the articulation of what one will do to, or make of, a work of art (or of, say, a third-grade portfolio, college term-paper, journal article, or NEH grant request) give us a standard, universal or otherwise, for reliably and responsibly assessing *processes* and *products*? We can move toward an answer by paying attention to verbs relating the creation, to making and doing (even, and especially, where the doing might be an undoing). For the art or act of creating is primal, archetypal, and fundamentally human—we might even say natural to us. The biological term "conception" finds an echo in philosophy; thus disciplines concerning the body and the mind come together at least here. This circular trick of language, by which ideas—like offspring— are conceived, is played out in many cultures. For example, to move toward primal origins: "Let there be . . . light." Here are words said to call into being life and light, understood as a shining forth in contrast to darkest oblivion; a bringing into being of something as opposed to nothing. Conception brings forth even as it is brought forth, for it too is called into being through language. And what of the root-word which draws life from the soil of language, "concept"? Let us consider the place of *concept* especially as it relates to arts related activities. Let us consider, in passing, the art of forming, inventing or fabricating concepts—as something done or made.

Philosophy is the discipline that involves *creating* concepts, which is to say (if somewhat circularly) of conceiving concepts (Deleuze and Guattari, 1994: 5). What does this mean, to conceive or create a concept? Can such a thing be done, let alone conceptualized? Can a concept be made? How is such a thing to be depicted, how marked, how modeled, or represented in or by means of art—or science? To be sure, science, art, and philosophy are all equally creative, but there is something about philosophy in the strict sense that makes the creation of concepts the province of that discipline, which is not to say that those who are engaged in arts related activities are not to some extent philosophers. And certainly, scientists are working with theories everyday that require conceptual leaps. At all events though: "Concepts are not waiting for us ready-made, like heavenly bodies. There is no heaven for concepts. They must be invented, fabricated, or rather created and would be nothing without their creator's signature" (Deleuze and Guattari, 1994: 5).

Nietzsche is credited as well with this conceptual breakthrough. In one of his more direct challenges to "re-evaluate all values," he outlines the rigorous task of anyone who would be a philosopher and not merely an academic laborer: "We must no longer accept concepts as a gift, nor merely purify and polish them, but first *make* and *create* them, present them and make them convincing. Hitherto one has generally trusted one's concepts as if they were a wonderful dowry from some sort of wonderland" (Nietzsche, 1968: 409). This famous passage is also cited and discussed by Deleuze and Guattari on their way to disclose the root of Hegel's powerful rendering of the idea of a concept as the philosophical reality of sense, where the concept is defined "by the Figures of its creation and the Moments of its self-positing" (Deleuze and Guattari, 1994: 5, 11).

We could dismiss Hegel entirely from this discussion were not for the remarkable influence that his ideas—and this one in particular—have had on generations of philosophers and art historians (whatever the extent to which they have been, if ever, truly understood as Hegel intended). And so, since I have been speaking of (and, perhaps, doing) philosophy, it is fitting at this stage in my analysis (regarding how we have come to speak of arts related activities in the West) to turn to Hegel. And, although this chapter makes no pretense to be a rigorous report on the history of Western metaphysics, but simply an exposé on the way words can conceal essential meanings, there are two things that need to be clarified before I can cite Hegel at length. First, for Hegel, beauty is a very complex concept. Essentially, though, beauty is understood to cut across and move beyond the sensual and the perceptual. Second, in adopting the expression "fine art," Hegel excludes the beauty of nature from his discussion altogether.

> Therefore the proper element of poetical representation is the poetical imagination and the illustration of spirit itself, and since this element is common to all the art forms, poetry runs through them all and develops itself independently in each of them. Poetry is the universal art of the spirit which has become free in itself and which is not tied down for its realization of external sensuous material; instead, it launches out exclusively in the inner space and the inner time of ideas and feelings. Yet, precisely, at this highest stage, art now transcends itself, in that it forsakes the element of a reconciled embodiment of the spirit in sensuous form and passes over from the poetry of the imagination to the prose of thought.

> This we may take to be the articulated totality of the particular arts: the external art of architecture, the objective art of sculpture, and the subjective art of painting, music, and poetry. But poetry is adequate to all forms of the beautiful and extends over all of them, because its proper element is beautiful imagination, and imagination is indispensable for every beautiful production, no matter to what form of art it belongs (Hegel, 1835/1975: 1, 89-90).

I would apologize for having to include so long a quotation but it is fundamental to what comes next, both with respect to the Western philosophical tradition and also my ensuing analysis. What we need to take with us though, as we proceed, is the notion that poetry (by which he means, *poesy*, the poetic imagination—the universal art of the spirit) is capable of embracing and taking on, and animating, all forms of the beautiful because it is the universal art of the spirit; it is not tied down to external sensuous material, the usual mediums of artistic endeavors and

related worldly stuff, for its realization. Through poetry then, art tran-
scends itself. Its destination is the beautiful imagination, and, on its
way, toward transcending itself, it leaves impressions of its passage on
certain forms to be seen here in the world.

Hegel developed these ideas at length in his monumental lectures on
aesthetics. For our purposes though we need keep in mind that, for Hegel
and thus for those who followed him, art is not the mere imitation of an
inert nature. Art is something else, and the work of art stands somewhere in the middle, as it were, between immediate sensuousness and
ideal thought. This concept, already carefully work out by Kant, was to
make Hegel's later work much easier for him. For Kant, in his description of the distinctions between agreeable and fine art, had asserted:

> it is fine art if its purpose is that the pleasure should accompany pre-
> sentations that are *ways of cognizing*. . . . Fine art . . . is a way of
> presenting that is purposive on its own and that furthers, even though
> without a purpose, the culture of our mental powers to [facilitate] so-
> cial communication. The very concept of the universal communicabil-
> ity of a pleasure carries with it [the requirement] that this pleasure
> must be a pleasure or reflection rather than one of enjoyment arising
> from mere sensation. Hence aesthetic art that is also fine art is one
> whose standard is the reflective power of judgment, rather than sensa-
> tion proper (Kant, 1790/1987: 172-73).

The overly precise language may seem a bit stilted to modern ears,
but it does succeed in conveying very distinctly a concept that came to be
an indispensable part of the tradition: the work of art comes between,
and in some cases can be said to mediate, immediate sensuousness and
ideal thought. From here it becomes possible to build a case for the
cognitive importance of art, which is precisely what Hegel did, by emphasizing art's historicity. In real terms this means that art can be
seen to develop teleologically, along a path ever toward its consumma-
tion—and in this it mirrors the principles of syntax underlying the construction of sentences. In the conclusion to this chapter, we will return to
Hegel's idea of history, though perhaps not in a way he would have
approved.

Hegel's ideas are still very much with us, whether or not we have
read (let alone understood) them, for they have influenced generations
of philosophers (and not a few academic laborers), critical theorists, and
art historians. Erwin Panofsky, who revolutionize twentieth century art

criticism by promoting an historically grounded approach to iconographic scholarship, put his spin on an essentially Hegelian view of the work of art in this way:

> In the case of a work of art, the interest in the idea is balanced, and may even be eclipsed by, an interest in form. However, the element of "form" is present in every object without exception, for every object consists of matter and form. . . . Anyone confronted with a work of art, whether aesthetically re-creating or rationally investigating it is affected by its three constituents: materialized form, idea (that is, in the plastic arts, subject matter) and content. . . . It is the unity of those three elements which is realized in the aesthetic experience, and all of them enter into what is called aesthetic enjoyment of art (Panofsky, 1955: 12, 16).

It was not so much the potential pleasure to be derived from the work of art (evident from Kant on) that troubled Heidegger, as it was the triad of form, idea, and content. He maintained that "form and content are the most hackneyed concepts under which anything and everything may be subsumed" (Heidegger, 1935-1936/1971: 27). So too Dewey was cautious in his use of such terminology: "The external object, the product of art, is the connecting link between artist and audience" (Dewey, 1934/1980: 106).

Concepts like form, idea, and content were not invented by Hegel, of course. And yet his indefatigable polishing of them endowed them with a sheen that many still see (and some are blinded by) today, and see in a way that eclipses the truth disclosed in and through the shining of the work of art. Still the concepts of form and content, at some juncture in the Western tradition, like any concept (as Deleuze and Guattari remarked), had to be invented, fabricated, created. With an eye toward personal experience within a community of those who create works of art that thus enable "esthetic experiences," Dewey maintained, "there can be no distinction, save between reflection, between form and substance. . . . The fact that form and matter are connected in a work of art does not mean they are identical (Dewey, 1934/1980: 109, 114). Further, according to the analysis of Herbert Marcus: "Aesthetic form is not opposed to content, not even dialectically. In the work of art, form becomes content and vice versa" (Marcuse, 1978: 41).

Such a view accords with the notion often attributed to Heidegger that there are no fixed centers or concepts such as "self" or "other" or "world" to which we can authentically anchor our philosophical systems. He takes another course; he chooses the middle ground, typical of the "middle-voice" he adopts when speaking of how things happen to be. Fundamental to his project is the creating of the concept that designates the being of Being, *Dasein* (literally, "being-there"). For our purposes it is enough to remark only that *Dasein* pertains to active engagement in the world, which is conceived of as being primarily a world of equipment or tools to *use* rather than a world of objects to *know*. It is here that we can begin to see with greater disclosive clarity Heidegger's originality in his effort to enable philosophy decisively to begin the overturning of itself—especially when we recall Kant's dictum that "it is fine art if its purpose is that the pleasure should accompany presentations that are *ways of cognizing*."

As it happens the conceptualization of the end of art that comes out of Heidegger's self-conscious philosophical project is not far from Dewey's democratizing vision of the order of things:

> A new poem is created by every one who reads poetically—not that its *raw* material is original for, after all, we live in the same old world, but that every individual brings with him, when he exercises his individuality, a way of seeing and feeling that in its interaction with old material creates something new, something previously not existing in experience (Dewey, 1934/1980: 108).

We are reminded here of Heidgger's understanding of *techne* denoting a mode of knowing, where knowing means to have seen in the widest sense of seeing, "which means to apprehend [to take hold of] what is present" (Heidegger, 1935-1936/1971: 59).

In line with this, Heidegger rejected the notion of truth as correspondence. Dewey replaced the idea of truth as correspondence to reality with "the idea of truth as what comes to be believed in the course of free and open encounters" (Rorty, 1989: 68). Despite the different and often convoluted paths they took to reach this conclusion, in the end, both Dewey and Heidegger rejected the notion of truth as correspondence. Dewey did so on his way to the determination of a pragmatic conception of objectivity. Heidegger did so in his following up the consequences of the truth in art as a truth that happens, that takes place in being set into the work of art, a truth therefore that is not *of* knowledge, and thus a notion of truth that more rightly could be called "double-truth" (Sallis,1995: 69). Even if the double ought not be called truth, still what remains decisive is the turn to that which grants truth: namely, the truth and the non-truth of disclosure that marks the condition of possibility of the truth or falsity of our propositions.

On this pivotal movement in Heidgger's thinking, John Sallis wrote: "It is this doubling that decisively breaks the bond of truth to knowledge in its traditional determination as intuition. For disclosedness is a matter neither *of* intuition nor *for* intuition. The originary phenomenon of truth, truth as disclosedness, is a truth that is not of knowledge" (Sallis, 1995: 68). This determination applies to words, no less than the work of art, for in everything that gets disclosed about the truth of the word, or the work of art, something else gets concealed or otherwise is allowed to recede. In "The Origin of the Work of Art" it comes out that "truth happens as the primal conflict between clearing and concealing," because every decision "bases itself on something not mastered, something concealed, confusing; else it would never be a decision. The earth is not simply the Closed but rather that which rises up as self-closing" (Heidegger, 1935-1936/1971: 55). And later in that same landmark essay on aesthetics, Heidegger talked about truth as disclosure—where there can be a "happening of truth at work" in a work of art, which opens up and discloses a world.

As we work through the following passage then, let us keep in mind that Heidegger's concept of double truth, in the end, enables him to gesture toward overturning the form of traditional metaphysical speculation, and thus toward rethinking the work of art outside its metaphysical end (where truth is conceived as correspondence, and art as being essentially mimetic). Also, Heidegger, with his characteristic philosophical rigor, acknowledges his starting point in Hegel's *Aesthetics*. Accordingly what is called "poesy" (or "poetry" as it is translated here), which runs through all of the arts, is to be understood as the universal art of the spirit. These are the terms he inherited and through which the discourse on the aesthetic experience and the origins of the work of art historically had been carried out. Heidegger takes off from here:

> The nature of art is poetry. The nature of poetry, in turn, is the founding of truth. We understand this founding here in a triple sense: founding as bestowing, founding as grounding, and founding as beginning. Founding however is actual only in preserving. . . . The founding of truth is a founding not only in the sense of free bestowal, but at the same time foundation in the sense of this ground-laying grounding. [. . .] Art is the setting-into-work of truth. In this proposition an

essential ambiguity is hidden, in which truth is at once the subject and the object of the setting. But subject and object are unsuitable names here. They keep us from thinking precisely about this ambiguous nature. . . . Art is historical, and as historical it is the creative preserving of truth in the work. Art happens as poetry. Poetry is founding in the triple sense of bestowing, grounding, and beginning. Art, as founding, is essentially historical. . . . Art lets truth originate. Art, founding preserving, is the spring that leaps to the truth of what is, in the work. To originate something by a leap, to bring something into being from out of the source of its nature in a founding leap—this is what the word origin (German *Ursprung*, literally, primal leap) means. [. . .] We inquire into the nature of art. Why do we inquire in this way? We inquire in this way in order to be able to ask more truly whether art is or is not an origin in our historical existence, whether and under what conditions it can and must be an origin (Heidegger, 1935-1936/1971: 75-78).

From here we can see our way more clearly toward turning the tables on traditional ways of speaking of art and arts related activities. Taking our lead from the careful analysis of the origin of the work of art as it relates to aesthetic experience, both on the part of Dewey with his social concerns and Heidegger with his historical ones, we can discern that the making of art is the happening of truth (even if it is a double truth). Further we can catch sight of the possibility that even as we may teach art (or philosophy, or biology, or literature, or feminist theory, or liberation theology, or calculus), and even though works of art may end up getting created (whether as a consequence of our class assignments, by accident or design; whether as a result of our own creative endeavors or those of our students), it is art that ends up literally creating us, historically, as a society that values what art is said to be and what art has to say about us.

* * * * *

Were it not for the work of John Sallis, I would not feel justified speaking of truth (double or otherwise), let alone shining truth, in this exposé of the way words can conceal essential meanings. Likewise the very use of terms like conceal take on new resonance when seen in terms of the double truth that comes out of Heidegger's work—which Sallis has explicated with great acumen (Sallis, 1995). Before his study of double truth though, Sallis performed another important service to philosophy in the West by reviving and resuscitating terms that had been all but banished from serious aesthetic studies decades ago, namely the terms "beauty" and "truth" (Sallis, 1994). He accomplished this by virtue of his decisive and critical marking of the term "shining" that belongs to art, and to philosophy, and to the ways we have come to speak about art and philosophy—and by extension, I would argue as well, education.

The crux to understanding his analysis is explained in the opening chapter of *Stone,* through a philological discussion of the Greek and German designations for beauty and light and shining. Hegel explicitly defined the beautiful as "the sensible shining of the idea [*das sinnliche Scheinen der Idee*]"; shining, therefore, names the way in which something beautiful offers itself to sense. Art is the sensible presentation of truth—that is, the presentation of truth in and through the shining of the work to sense (Sallis, 1994: 3) Building on Hegel's work in this field, from which Heidegger ventured to derive "the *truth* of art" where beauty is to be thought "as a way of shining," the work of art gives place to truth, indeed it "provides the place where truth can appear, can shine" (Sallis, 1994: 4). Sallis leaps on ahead further by invoking the question posed by Heidegger in *The Origin of the Work of Art* about Hegel's *Aesthetics*, the unsettled question of whether art is past—or, put differently, in the words of Heidegger's Epilogue: "is art still an essential and necessary way in which that truth happens which is decisive for our historical existence, or is art no longer of this character?" Hegel had concluded that art's form, in the emergent Industrial Age, had ceased to be the highest need of the spirit, and that: "In all these relationships art is and remains for us, on the side of its highest vocation, something past."

Maurice Blanchot likewise sees this as the ground zero for any future any inquiry that seeks to get beyond the posing of the question. And so he asks "But why this question?"—namely: *L'art est-il chose passé?* [Is art something that is done?] (Blanchot, 1993: 282, 288-89). Blanchot takes Hegel at his word, and hears in his words a dictum. As such he seeks to hear in the French verb "passer" something that is over and finished, and which is marked as such both by grammar (the *past* tense) and by culture (for us, now, it is done): "L'art est pour nous chose passée" (Blanchot, 1993: 284). What is it about this question that marks it as being fundamentally a question of and about our culture—or rather of what has passed, and passes now, as our culture? To ask whether art is something that for us is past, returns us to the pragmatic perspective of art as a thing ("something in order to").

By the same token teachers speak, often without stopping to remark on the singularity of the expression, of passing (or not passing) students, whether referring to a test, course, or entire grade. Many colleges today allow students to take at least course risk-free, as it were, so as to encourage them to pursue something outside their area of specialization but which cannot hurt their over all GPA—and all that this entails. In some schools this "Pass/Fail" option is referred to as "Pass/Not Pass," which implicitly acknowledges, though hardly does away with, the stigma attached to the word "Fail." It is common to speak of "passing grades" as an index to a student's having met at least the minimum standards. But in such a passing we can hear both in the language itself and in the school culture that perpetuates it, a decisive if unreflective articulation of *would-be* overcoming, of moving on and beyond what one was before because of something extrinsic: a teacher, a test, a school board, a tenure committee has judged and spoken. You pass the third grade and go on to the fourth, and in so doing are told that you have moved beyond what you were before. What though is truly being done here? None of this, of course, takes into account the hotly contested issue of standardized testing used to determine whether a student passes from one tier to the next (Kohn, 2000; Ohanian, 1999), as this represents a domain of thought and activity beyond the borders of what has been mapped out for this book [FIGURE 0.2].

But why is it that we have not overcome this way of thinking and speaking about art no less than about grades? Has language alone kept it in the realm of useful things? In this regard can it be said that language draws culture? To what end and along what way does it drag culture?

Is art, then, something that is for us over, something done, something that has passed along the way; that has passed away? And, if so, then what manner of thing is this Art that we are talking about? To say *"We had art yesterday"* implies that the event, the experience (like a class session or a chapter), lasted for a while and then was over. Does anything linger? Does anything remain though once you are done with it and the product stands on its own, no longer able to receive or submit to the artist's finishing touches? And so: What part does being finished with a work (of art or of philosophy) play in its life? Whether as creator, consumer, or destroyer: To what extent is the prospective "being finished" present at the inception, in the very conception, of a work of art, so much so that it is irrevocably conditioned and shaped and informed by this legacy? What, if anything, lingers from the experience? What makes possible the sensible shining of the idea? After all is said and done: What sustains the shining in and through the world that is opened up by virtue of the work of art, which gives place to truth and provides the place where truth can appear, can shine? Through its shining, the work of art can let truth be, can let truth appear; and yet it is the sensible shining character of the art-work that destines art to have become something past (Sallis, 1994: 43-44).

It is in this light I pause to consider that learning outcomes essentially are things that are done; a finished product is, by its very definition (and mandate), over; it is done. It is the character of work-products to call to mind, though it may leave no discernible trace of, the process that brought it into being. For whatever the reasons, *products*, often interpreted as "results," are what tend to be valued in our culture—whether in juried art-shows, classroom instruction, or corporate balance sheets (the latter can refer to institutions of higher learning no less than *Fortune* 500 companies). What is done, and that which is shown, tend to take precedence over other kinds of shining forth and bringing to presence the truth of art. Correlatively, what are we to make of the fact that the sanctioned aim of the doing of art (or of philosophy, of literature, of theorizing critically about any or all of these normative disciplines), that the prized end of the creative process, tends to be a finished product to which others, in turn, can react, can respond—whether they accept or reject it, imitate or deride it, praise or co-opt it?

Perhaps this is the result of a confusion regarding the end (or goal) of what is done in the doing of that which enables and discloses the happening of truth in a work of art. It is characteristic of art to be involved with what is past, with what is over and done. In German the word is *vorbei* and as a noun *das Vorbei* names death (Sallis, 1994: 30-31). In the doing of art then, art keeps running up against its own prospective passing, its own incipient gone-ness. Even so, in and through the doing of art also comes the possibility of the sensible shining that is truth; the possibility of art that comes to pass (and yet which is thereby destined to pass away) as the happening of truth.

Art is involved with what is over and done, with what already has been anticipated and completed—whether on the one hand a product that becomes part of one's *oeuvre*, portfolio, or resume; or, on the other, something like a bold conception, a cunning design, a fleeting image, a concept created. . . . Perhaps then, keeping in mind the notion of double truth and the possibilities is allows, we can celebrate rather than fear

what may well be the most paradoxical of our many conflicting charges
as artists, as students, as teachers: to make sure that art is not done.

* * * * *

As a way to reach for a conclusion that remains true to the terms and
argument of the exposé just presented, I would loop back to the Introduction and, back further still, to the epigraph page so as to twist free of
this chapter and leap ahead to what comes next. In doing so I would ask
you to reflect on what was said in the opening of this chapter about
decoration: "Why is art so quickly coded as being mere decoration, or
made the province of what a handful of gifted draftsmen can do because
of their innate abilities to represent recognizable things?" With this in
mind, I would move closer to an end by repeating, by recycling, the
words of another regarding what is to be done with the work of art that
we ourselves are. Each one of us:

> must organize the chaos within him by thinking back to his real needs.
> His honesty, the strength and truthfulness of his character, must at
> some time or other rebel against the state of things in which he only
> repeats what he has heard, learns what is already known, imitates what
> already exists; he will then begin to grasp that culture can be some-
> thing other than a decoration of life, that is to say at bottom no more
> than dissimulation and disguise; for all adornment conceals that which
> is adorned (Nietzsche, 1874/1999: 123).

These words give a practical reason to take to heart Bakunin's maxim
about the desire to rebel. In rebelling against the state of things in which
one repeats only what one has heard, one can come to organize the chaos
within and perhaps also that which is outside of us, in the communities
of which we are a part. This is especially the case where education is
concerned. And so, what one gets from a poem, painting, or treatise—
whether as creator, consumer, or destroyer—, what one gets from a
lesson, grade in school, or college education—whether as bystander,
conduit, or conductor—, depends on the extent to which one has recognized, and perhaps managed to organize or at least rechannel, the chaos
that drives our relationship to teaching and to learning.

Whether or not our relation to art and to the culture of education is
expressed in terms of, and thus is drawn by, language, learning need not
be mere decoration. Ornamentation, as Nietzsche proposes, tends to

conceal. This chapter has been about disclosure and disclosiveness. In it I have pushed to counter a view of pragmatic aesthetics that wrongly (1) focuses on products, learning outcomes, and so on, by reifying artistic and philosophical activity; and (2) is superficial about truth, conceiving it as correspondence, not as disclosive of self, other, and the world. I am driven to do this out of my experience with second-graders who, as makers of art, are practicing becoming creative disclosers of world and self; as such they are participating in, and are co-effected by, the happening of truth. This much having being seen, we can proceed now to look toward what it is then that shines forth in the world opened up by the work of art that teaching is and which it makes possible—a world in which learning can be said to happen.

# Chapter 4

## What Can Be Taught

### I. Preamble

Just as there are limits to what can be thought, there are limits to what can be taught. Can ethics be taught? Based on my experience teaching courses called "Ethics," I would answer: No. Ethics cannot be taught, even though, to be sure, moral behavior can be learned (Brandt, 1959).

A course in Spinoza's *Ethics* or Aristotle's *Nicomachean Ethics* can be taught in many settings other than a philosophy class. By the same token, literature courses often concern the deeds and sayings of exemplary figures, of heroes and villains. Courses can be taught in business or medical ethics, and the fact that such offerings are cropping up in many institutions across the country is a telling sign of the times (Garber et al., 2000). The prevalence of such courses no doubt stems from many motives, not the least of which is a school or professional society needing to show the world they take the topic seriously. It is also generally acknowledged that students and professionals alike need to be familiar with the sorts of things typically covered in such courses if they are to be competitive enough to enter their chosen field and then to compete responsibly and successfully within it (Bellah et al., 1985/1996), whether business, medicine, law, conservation, social work, art, military science, software design, teaching, or coaching.

The problem with the way the initial question was posed ("Can ethics be taught?") is that it puts a heavy burden on the verb "teach," and subsequently on the role of the teacher, more fitting of, say, "mentor." But this chapter is not about what words disclose or conceal about their meanings and how this shapes our activities in the world—ethical or otherwise. This chapter concerns "What can be taught" as a theme, and also posed as a question: "What can be taught?"

My first encounter with this line of inquiry came unexpectedly. Once during an "office hours round-table," which I hosted weekly for students to raise issues perhaps not suited to regular class discussion, Anil Gocklani told me "you're teaching us ethics, you know." I did not know that was what I was doing. I thought I had been teaching him literature, another fencing, and the third student philosophy in an independent reading course. If they were correct, then was it an appropriate thing for me to be doing—teaching them ethics—when they were supposed to be learning to read Milton, to parry a thrust, to think bravely with Nietzsche's Zarathustra? If this was something they were getting on their own in addition to what I was obliged contractually to teach them, then was it OK? But, I wondered further: Am I capable of teaching in such a way so that I am *not* teaching ethics? I had to answer: No (and this is still my answer today). This may contradict what I said at the beginning of the chapter. If it does, then it is a contradiction on the order of those contraries I mentioned in the Introduction (especially the closing paragraph), which I have had to acknowledge, embrace, analyze, and seek to resolve—or at least try to keep in balance.

To say that we are never too old to learn ethics (Parks, 1993: 13) assumes that ethics can be taught. A teacher can say she is teaching ethics, but what tests can be used to determine whether ethics have been learned? How long after the lesson does it take before consistent and persistent moral behavior can be demonstrated? Are extreme situations that cut to the marrow of one's being required to test the true extent to which one has mastered valid ethical principles? While the instrumental value of providing people with the motivation to meet the demands of the core content of morality should be obvious, intrinsically valuable feelings of, say, belonging, friendship, and solidarity may not be so obvious and easy to assess (Jones, 1999: 59). And so, despite programs specifically designed to determined relative successes in this regard, the proverbial jury is still out on whether ethics is as much an attitude as it is a set of skills (Piper, 1993: 119). And this brings me to a second occasion when I was able to confront my problem with teaching ethics, when I became a registered provider of courses in "Ethics and Professionalism" monitored by the Tennessee Commission on Legal Education and Specialization (CLE&S, or CLE for short).

Lawyers across America are compelled to go to classes much in the same way traditional students are who want a diploma attesting to their special abilities or technical skills. Earning a credential may or may not have anything to do with whether the student actually learned what the teacher thought he was teaching. There are many ways to get certified nowadays so as to enter the work force ready for whatever comes, and able to compete on equal footing with others seeking the same position. In an educational utopia, teachers would have willing students who are eager to learn and capable of formulating original research projects. In the real world, however, teachers work with students who are compelled to be in the classroom, whether by virtue of intrinsic or extrinsic goals, motives, or pressures. Undoubtedly the joy of learning plays a part in some students' lives. But, more times than not, we have students who would rather be somewhere else—perhaps in another class, already at the job they seek, having coffee or a beer with friends, spending time with children, or, quite simply, be anywhere else but in our class.

Continuing education courses, like all forms of classroom instruction, run best when the teacher acknowledges and respects the specific needs and goals of the students. This is especially true when teaching professionals who have all worked very hard to get where they are. We need to take into account and respect such students' status as authorities in their respective fields while at the same time recognizing they may be a long way from their experiences with general education. And yet, to use the example of CLE requirements, if they hope to maintain their licenses to practice law in the state, they must annually attend classes in "Continuing Legal Education"; in Tennessee this means fifteen credit hours, three of which must concern "Ethics and Professionalism." This particular situation raises a series of questions that have larger ramifications than merely the mandate of continuing legal education. The questions it raises will help me bring into focus *the moral component implicit in any educational delivery system.*

Before going into those questions though, let me first loop back to and add two more things to the Credo from Chapter 2. First, I believe it is the duty of the teacher to look beyond the surface of the material that is expected to be conveyed to or (as the saying has it) drilled into the student; and, whenever possible, to bring this to the attention of one's students by reflecting purposefully on the broader implications of what it is they are committed to learning and how you intend to go about teaching this to them. Second, I believe that no matter what the material we teach, we must make it our duty to draw out questions implicitly posed by our subject matter as well as regarding how we go about teaching it. We must seek to respond to such questions professionally and with care, just as we would respond to questions posed to us by our students. In everyday terms, such considerations make me reflect on how I can get my students certified while teaching them what they need to know to advance creatively in their areas of interest or profession (and at times, though of course not always, these overlap), and also to make sure they take something away with them of lasting moral value. If this is tantamount to teaching ethics, then I am guilty as charged.

After all, ethics, broadly speaking, informs everything we do in the classroom; for example, how we treat our students, the honesty with which we assess every student's needs and abilities, how we comport ourselves with our peers. It would seem also that ethics, whether we are aware of it or not, pervades all that we do in the world, whether professionally or domestically. Some people speak of a work-ethic, meaning how they go about meeting obligations in a timely and honorable way; others speak of the ethics of this or that approach to a problem since every situation is different and requires different standards for evaluating appropriate behavior.

What I have in mind though is ethics in a more pure sense, and I am using the term pure according to its basic philosophical understanding, as that which legislates *a priori*—by reasoning from cause to effect, deductively (Kant, 1790/1987: 16-19). To get at what some of the principles underlying such a conception of pure ethics might be, let me at last pose the series of questions that brings into focus the moral component implicit in any educational deliver system.

First, if I offer a course for lawyers titled "Ethics and Professionalism," should it be my goal to make my students aware of ethical issues (and the problems surrounding them that they may not previously have recognized as such) or to make them more ethical? The former seems more realistic; the latter impossible to monitor. And yet is it enough that the lawyer, as an officer of the court, upholds the laws as written? Can what passes as sound ethical principles be universalized, let alone taught to students the same way every time? What can we do to enable our students to become cognizant of these sorts of questions and the problems they represent, and thus to help them identify and secure for themselves a place (albeit provisionally) on the moral continuum? Do such considerations contradict the call to "re-evaluate all values" discussed in Chapter 3? If so, then the rest of this chapter seeks to broker a truce between the two contrary positions; or, at least, to entertain the possibility that tradition and innovation, that education and anarchy, dance hand in hand if learning is destined to occur. I will present three possible itineraries, which collectively can be seen as an attempt to engage and question what our cognitive powers can accomplish when confronted with a domain of instruction that I maintain, *a priori*, does not actually have quantifiable objects of knowledge. Such is the realm of ethics.

## II. Three Possibilities

The first section, "Literature and Human Values," originally was proposed to a computer-manufacturing company for its team managers and floor workers. I have modified the program somewhat so it can be applied to other kinds of continuing education venues as well. The second way I explore the issue of whether and the extent to which ethics can be taught comes from a series of seminars designed for staff members in government offices; a program aptly called "Educating the Princes." And finally, the third and final part of my critique regarding the teaching of ethics takes the form of a series of seminars presented to a law firm, advertised simply as "Books with Bill."

All of these courses were for people already integrated into the work place and who had completed their formal education. Some, I learned later, were planning to get more training and additional credentials down the road in areas pertinent to their aspirations. These courses therefore had less to do with *schooling* and more to do with *education*. The main differences between the two can be seen at a glance (though pondered at length) using a handy set of mnemonic word strings: TEST for *schooling* and EVER for *education* [FIGURE 4.1 and FIGURE 4.2]. And yet, for teachers who are obliged contractually—and who perhaps feel morally bound—to give students grades and to "rank them," the question of what can be taught (and of what can *possibly* be taught—let alone thought) when you are required to TEST, really boils down to: How do you do what is implied by FIGURE 4.2 when you have to do what is implied by FIGURE 4.1.

## Figure 4.1

**SCHOOLING** tends to be *place specific* and *temporally limited.*

The student tends to be managed, processed, and "taught to"...

$T$AUGHT --› *t*eacher-based {Formulae:

Applications

Software

Technical info

$E$ VALUATED --› *e*conomic model (curve + grade = rank)

$S$TAMPED --› tran*s*cript is marked "official" and then, you are

$T$OSSED OUT --› in*t*o the World & job *market*: "Dear Alum"

**Figure 4.2**

**EDUCATION** can take place *anywhere* and happen at *anytime*.

With the process of learning being paramount, students encounter:

$E$NRICHMENT --› {Learning how to learn:

Info to make your way in the world,

Finer things that seem to matter to you, &

Everything else still to be encountered;

$V$ALUES --› {Challenged,

Affirmed,

Reinforced,

Exchanged;

$E$NTERTAINMENT --› element of *play*; the joy of learning;

$R$ESPECT --› {Respect  for

Environment,

Self,

Property,

Everyone else,

Community,

Traditions.

# 1. Literature and Human Values

"Literature and Human Values" provides a forum for your teams to come together once (or twice) a month for stress-free encounters with works of great literature. In addition to entering into dialogue with the likes of Plato, Shakespeare, and Goethe, participants will gain insight into their co-workers' points of view and come to learn more about and, it is hoped, appreciate their differences. The readings will be especially selected so as to take into account the various backgrounds of your staff and to match the goals of your mission statement. They follow a course that will enable participants to see connections between and among the texts, and then to make the leap out from them to everyday concerns. No previous background in the selected works is expected and no preparation for the seminar is required. The reading selection will be distributed after lunch, during which time I will give a brief and lively survey of the book and the author's life and times. Participants then will take turns reading short passages from a manageable portion of the selected work, followed by questions and discussion. Through this format, participants are equipped and encouraged to return on their own to the complete text or others by the same author, and to continue living with the ideas and issues raised in the seminar.

The service provided by "Literature and Human Values" has benefits beyond intellectual enrichment and the cultivation of collegiality. Most notably, participants will be better able to recognize, address, and to head-off potential conflicts. This is a result of the approach to encountering works of literature I have adopted, which draws freely and widely from the vast reservoir of examples and counter-examples in the world's great literary traditions and also those available to us in contemporary life and culture. Literature, while a social institution, is also a mirror of the world in all of its variety; and it can show us how we can live more deliberately and reflectively. A typical seminar might find us encountering twelve authors (whether one or two a month, to be determined in the participants):

Plato, *Republic*, Book VII; Aristotle, *Ethics*, Book I
Cicero, *The Good Life;* Seneca, *Epistles*
Petrarch, sonnets; Machiavelli, *The Prince*
Montaigne, *Essays*, Book II; Spenser, *Faerie Queene*, Book V
Shakespeare, *Pericles*; Goethe, *Faust, Part I*
Gogal, *Dead Souls;* poems by Whitman, Frost, Levertov

Although the regular day, time, and place of the meeting can be determined by the group or a supervisor, I would recommend that it convene in a conference room where, or not far from where, the participants work together everyday. Books and learning need not be disassociated from one's place of business. Further, it is hoped that positive experiences with the Humanities will carry over into everything we do in our daily lives. Follow-up seminars are available for, once one is familiar with and used to the joy of learning made possible through living with great books, there can be no end to lifelong learning [see again FIGURE 4.2].

## 2. Educating the Princes

The spirit and aims of this program are consistent with Renaissance Humanism. The Renaissance has been admired for the great changes it witnessed in society and government, and for vast achievements in the arts and science. And while Humanism was the main current of thought during the Renaissance, it still has many practical applications. Originally it was a specific intellectual program, and only incidentally did it suggest the more general set of values that in recent times have come to be called humanistic. These are the values, especially as pertains to civic virtue and enlightened statecraft, I intend to revive and present for the consideration of staff members working with policy-makers in our government offices today.

Renaissance Humanism was the outgrowth of the earlier traditions of professional teaching, with an emphasis on classical studies. At first the focus was on how texts had been transmitted and on the form and style of those texts. Soon however Humanists came to give equal attention to the noble deeds and sayings of the ancients so that they, and their students, could get their moral bearings. This is the case as well for the program proposed here.

The interests of the original Humanists ranged from rhetoric and poetry to history and moral philosophy, and the disciplines that allowed the proper study of these things came to be known collectively as *Studia Humanitatis*, or the Humanities (Cassirer et al., 1948: 4). Although this is merely another name for these particular studies, the choice to collect them under one heading, in a single term, Humanities, implies something very characteristic about the cultural and educational ideals of the Humanists themselves: namely, that the cultivation of the classics, of the Humanities, is justified because it serves to educate and produce a desirable type of human being. The Humanities then represent the highest level of human achievement, and should be of primary concern to everyone.

The Humanist's goal was to further the Humanities, and thereby to improve society. He did so by seeking out future statesmen who wanted to deepen and broaden the base of their learning beyond the specialized training they had received in law or diplomacy, in finance or administration. The rationale was simple: by educating the princes, society would be improved. For proof of its effectiveness, we need only look to the enduring achievements in art, architecture, and literature that came out of the Italian Renaissance. What we remember most from this epoch is not what party or leader was supreme at what time, but rather the masterpieces created and architectural monuments commissioned as a result of the even-handed legislation and open-handed patronage of those same princes. So too my goal is to provide an opportunity for today's princes to become re-immersed in Humanistic values and to refine their own understandings of the value of the Humanities. Our modern day princes are those men and women who, by a combination of good fortune, hard work, and their own determination, are seeking to put a guiding hand on the tiller of the ship of state.

I encourage students to keep in mind what they should be able to do with what they are learning. And so I have developed techniques for helping them reflect on and build beyond what they already know. At the same time I advocate that we must take each book on its own terms, and then determine how to transfer its perennial lessons into practical, everyday thinking and action. This is the essence of my teaching, coupled with my belief that not much ever really is learned when a student is made to feel she or he needs to defer to an authority (or teacher) every step of the way. Consequently, drawing on my experience as a close reader of the classics, I make available a variety of time-tried approaches, presented in a fresh and memorable and often humorous way, so that the students on their own can unearth the treasures waiting for them in the works we study. This approach makes it more likely that they will understand the work from the inside out, and then apply whatever lessons are to be learned in their own lives.

The plan I propose is consistent with the pragmatic ideals and theoretical objectives of Renaissance Humanism. Therefore, like the Humanists of old, we can learn much from venerating the classics even as we strive to work with them in ways that are appropriate to the concerns and affairs of contemporary life. To accommodate schedules of the twelve staff members in the Washington, D.C. area taking part in our six-week seminar, we will meet one evening a week for ninety minutes. During the meetings we will determine a context for our discussion (perhaps based on issues in the news), and then read from the following books:

(1) Cicero, *Of Duties;* Plutarch, *Morals*
(2) Dante, *Inferno* and *On Monarchy*
(3) Chaucer, select *Canterbury Tales*
(4) Sackville, *Mirror for Magistrates*
(5) Machiavelli, *Discourses*; Bacon, *Essays*
(6) Shakespeare, *Measure for Measure*

My objective in setting up the program this way is to get the group actively involved with larger ideas and noble ideals, which in large measure account for the enduring value of these books. Beyond the obvious intellectual benefits of such a course of study there is also the possible outcome, that the values discussed in our seminars somehow will get translated into the participants' daily life. Further, participants will come to know more about, and to respect, the differing beliefs and values of their co-workers. This will engender a sense of *esprit de corps* while renewing an abiding love of learning that we all have experienced at some point in our schooling and, it is hoped, outside of and beyond our schooling as well [see again FIGURE 4.2].

## 3. Books with Bill

I began each of the sessions for this law firm with a reminder of the format and main objectives: "to give some background, have us read a manageable selection from a landmark book, and to provide an opportunity for questions and answers so that, later, on your own, you will be equipped and ready to return to the complete text or others by the author, and to continue to live with the ideas presented—as you understand them—and make them part of your life." To give a better sense of how such an approach can be used, let me present three sets of lesson plans, each of which followed the same basic pattern: a consideration of why this selection historically has been considered a great book or benchmark text; the context of how it came to be written; situating the excerpt in the scheme of the larger work; a reading of the passage aloud by participants (selections are determined by lottery); and then going over prepared questions followed by a general discussion.

## *Socrates/Plato*

It is hard to live in the West and not have at least heard of Socrates and Plato, and the "wisdom of the Ancient Greeks"; but perhaps we haven't had much contact with them in a while, or never got around to reading them as closely as we might have liked. Whether we are aware of it or not, our own thinking owes a great deal to Plato, so that it makes sense we should go back and see what he actually said. After all Augustine especially in his *City of God*, a foundational text of early Christianity, is everywhere indebted to Platonic ideas and the separating of the invisible world of spirit and light from that of the visible world of matter and appearances. His theology is a masterfully reworking of Plato's themes: Augustine puts "God" where Plato had placed "Good," though the intellectual framework remains to a large extent in tact. Likewise, early Judaism owes much to the Platonising tendencies of the great Talmudic scholars and exegetes. The same is true of Islam, especially during the five centuries of its expansion during the Middle Ages which led to a great flourishing of art and literature, as well as remarkable advances in medicine, astronomy, and mathematics. And so, of all of the works of Plato that I might have selected, I took a passage from Book VII of *The Republic* because it stands as one of the most concise expositions of his thought. In it we find Plato's entire system folded into a single, simple "allegory of a cave." To have read this allegory closely, and to have read it well, is to have made a valuable and enduring inroad into Plato's thought; for, as Alfred North Whitehead once put it: Western philosophy is but footnotes to Plato.

[I presented explanatory mind-maps, a chronological table, and an overview of Athenian democracy to the group. But since any standard edition of Plato will have a good bare-bones treatment of the dialogue and a sketch of the author's life and times, and since my lecture notes were geared to a specific kind of audience, I have refrained from reproducing all of the materials I used for the seminar. Instead I give only the topic-questions used to stimulate discussion, so as to suggest some possible ways that ethics can be approached in the classroom, if not taught.]

A) What would Socrates/Plato have us do to lead the "good life"?

B) After all, Plato uses the same tricks of rhetoric familiar to "The Sophist." His whole argument hinges on allegory—on images and metaphors—which, by his own admission, are "shadowy." And yet what is it about his approach, and the story itself, that keep it from being more than an exercise in sophistry?

C) If you had managed to get out of the Cave, would you go back to tell the others what you had seen and try to get them to come back out with you? What methods of persuasion might you use? What would compel you? Why not just go up into the Light and make a new life for yourself?

D) Is it really as easy to be fooled by appearances as Plato suggests? What about in the Moral World (of Good and Evil)— don't we just know when something is wrong?

E) How would Plato account for the fact that we can know the better and still do the worse? How would you explain it?

F) Is the purpose of education, as Plato suggests, to draw people out of the dark (ignorance) and into the Light? To what end?

G) The *Republic* gives us one of the earliest "utopias" in European literature and confronts the modern reader with arguably the ultimate problem of political life: How can the state be so ordered as to place effective control in the hands of people who understand that you cannot make either an individual or a society happy by making them richer or more powerful than their neighbors? How then is happiness tied in with recognizing and doing what is "right"?

H) The main questions to be answered in the *Republic* are: What does Justice mean, and how can it be realized in human society? Socrates' utopian vision is not offered as a viable model, though it does stand as a projection upward and outward of what Justice (and just conduct) might resemble. So the larger questions before us now are: What is justice, and how can we help bring it about in our daily lives?

## Cervantes

While there are earlier romances and prose narratives, the novel (in the modern sense of the term) begins with *Don Quixote*. It is perhaps the most talked about though least read famous work of literature, and other

than the Bible no single work has been translated into as many languages. What is it about this novel that captures the imagination of people
worldwide since the date when it was written? Is it simply to "reach the
unreachable star"? Is it the charming characterization of man who has
read too much and comes to believe the world is a copy of art? A mod-
ern-day equivalent might be the person who thinks that social relations
mirror, and can be understood by watching, soap operas and sit-coms.

Though we have all heard of the episode of the deranged knight
tilting at windmills that he sees as—or wants to believe are—giants, we
may not know much else about the novel, except perhaps that Don
Quixote's side-kick, his squire, is named Sancho Panza. These two un-
likely compatriots—the impossibly thin, melancholy, and idealistic knight
who imagines the most commonplace things to be the stuff of great and
chivalrous adventures; and the rotund, sanguine, and earthy squire who
wants to get as much out of the travels as he can grab on the go. Together they make up a more complete portrait of humanity, each needs
the other for balance. Each is incomplete without the other. But the
novel lines up other points of balance as well, by showing them as im-
balances. In this work, as in the others read during the course of our
seminars, the issue of how we conceptualize social justice is central to
understanding authority, especially where personal conduct is concerned.
And so, among the recurring quirky features of *Don Quixote* that we
encounter along the way, the character of the author and the origins of
the book are discussed and debated both from within framework of the
book as well as among critics.

The selected passage (Part I, chapter 22, "Of the freedom Don Quixote
conferred on many unfortunate persons who against their will were being taken where they did not want to go") brings out these themes and
larger social questions. In this, it is perhaps more representative of the
novel as a whole than the celebrated windmill episode. Like most of the
episodes, this one concludes with hero and squire being drubbed nearly
to death, misunderstood (or understood all too well), and not really learning anything from their experience. But what do we learn here?

[As with the previous example, once again to encourage you to consider and perhaps to develop your own approach to whether ethics can be
taught, I have not reproduced the materials used to convey the historical
setting of both book and author. However, as before, by way of example, I give below the eight topic questions, which indicate the goals of
"Books with Bill."]

A) In his own mind, Don Quixote can rationalize releasing the prisoners. In taking the law into his own hands for what he deems to be a greater good, he resembles not only a noble, if fictitious, chivalric character but also a vigilante-marauder. Is this a case of his doing the wrong thing for what he believes are the right reasons? After all he is rightly punished (by the wrong people) for his crime. Recalling that Cervantes had been a slave himself and had liberated galley slaves, what other message might be found (hidden) here? When is it OK to take the law into your own hands? Where is the line drawn?

B) Ginés is like Don Quixote (and Cervantes). Among other things, they are both clever and unfortunate ("Misfortune always persecutes good wit"). Is he a foil for Don Quixote? A sinister parallel? Why do the men follow Ginés? What lesson is drawn about "authority"?

C) There is a lot of violence, some good-natured and some not so good-natured, in this novel. What are to make of the drubbing that Sancho and Don Quixote receive?

D) What sort of laughter is elicited by the knight's antics? In what ways is his adherence to the idealism of chivalry endearing and charming? In what ways chilling and scary?

E) Giné's crime is never specified, but what sort of misdeeds might he be guilty of "worse than those of all the others put together" (as the guard puts it to Don Quixote)? What sorts of crimes is an author guilty of when he relates "facts so neat and amusing that no lies could match them"? When does telling the truth deserve punishment?

F) What is it that really gets to Don Quixote and makes him free the prisoners? Is he brave?

G) What might have been the result of the prisoners doing as Don Quixote asked: returning to Dulcinea del Toboso and telling her of the noble deeds of their liberator and her admirer? What is the end result of two such varied worldviews colliding in broad daylight, and what does Cervantes have in mind in wanting us to consider such an eventuality but not actually hearing it narrated in detail?

H) Unlike other episodes in *Don Quixote*, this one finds the Knight of Sad Countenance (as he likes to be known), listening more than talking, hearing new names given to things rather than giving fantastic explanations to mundane occurrences. Here he speaks less, and acts more; but, as in all other episodes, he still ends up acting in accordance with his romance-oriented world-view. Likewise, Sancho does not get many good lines in this chapter; he just observes everything from his earthy and simple perspective. This chapter then is a kind of counter-balance to the usual plotting of the novel, and as such it enables the characteristic ebb and flow of the peculiar and original narrative design. What might Cervantes have in mind by letting these convicted criminals dominate the discourse, with the permission of Don Quixote (and the guard) to tell their stories? What is the importance of the telling and of the hearing of such stories? With whose words are such stories related and what is the impact of those words—in the world of the novel, and also in the world? Put differently: What do words avail once "sentence" has been passed?

## *Machiavelli*

Over time his name has become synonymous with cunning, usually underhanded, policy; getting what you want, at whatever the cost, and no matter who gets in your way. A "Machiavelle," though, is always the "other guy" for we, ourselves, of course, are clear of such practices. *The Prince*, out of the many books written during the Italian Renaissance, most thoroughly ushers in modern political thought. As Ernst Cassirer wrote with characteristic acumen: With Machiavelli we stand at the gateway of the modern world (Cassirer, 1973: ch.12). But what is it, exactly, that is so modern and innovative about Machivelli's thought?

To regard *The Prince* as an ethical treatise is impossible. It is neither a moral nor an immoral work; it is, rather, as some have suggested, a technical book. In this regard it stands out as a literary and philosophical innovation. Because of its use of historical precedents to convey the author's recurring theme, in previous days such a book would have been seen as a text on moral philosophy. In effect though this book looks beyond the facile categories of hero and villain, of good and of evil.

Perhaps it is for this reason that Machiavelli was much admired by Nietzsche, who praised him for his direct style and honest narrative about human nature (Nietzsche, 1956).

But pushing even beyond this, it is instructive for our purposes to see *The Prince* as a technical manual or even as a scientific book. We are invited to read it today in the same way we might approach a computer start-up manual: We do not seek moral advice from it, nor do we look for good or evil. It is enough if we are told what is useful, what works and what doesn't. The author speaks as if with an entirely detached and objective mind. Still, as Cassirer has argued, it remains one of the great puzzles in the history of human civilization how a man like Machiavelli, a great and noble mind, could become an advocate of splendid wickedness. The puzzle becomes even more bewildering still when we compare *The Prince* with his other writings, especially *Discourses on Livy* in which his sympathy clearly is on the side of the common people (Cassirer, 1973: chapter 12).

Machiavelli's judgment, it has been said, was that of a scientist and a technician of political life; this is what he knew by training and trade. After he had been removed from a position of authority though, he never again held public office even though he spent the rest of his life in hope of someday being reinstated. Luckily for posterity, his talents were elsewhere. His direct and incisive observations anticipate the maxims and essays of Bacon and the coming of the New Science. If we read *The Prince* otherwise, we lose the gist of the whole matter as it is presented.

In *The Prince*, in brief, actions, whether of an individual or group, are the result of motivations that can be rationally explained. Whether we like it or not, Machiavelli threw down a gauntlet "which subsequent writers on statecraft have found it almost impossible to ignore" (Skinner and Price, 1989: xxiv). Indeed, Machiavelli's basic assumption is asserted more as a debating proposition than as a fact: Whether it is the case that leaders must always be prepared to do evil if they think good will come of it. Therefore the excerpted passages selected for "Books with Bill" are those that most succinctly express this theme (chapters 9-10, 15, 17-18) and which, in the process, confront head-on the assumption upon which the treatise is based.

[Insofar as any recent edition of *The Prince* will give a chronology that can be used to situate the historical circumstances leading to its composition and dedication, as before, I will forego reproducing my resource materials. I would, however, ask you to keep in mind that this way of teaching the book is different from how it was discussed in Chapter 2. Irrespective of how one approaches this book though, the question (to which I will return when next I teach *The Prince*) remains whether or not it might in fact exceed the limits of what can be thought.]

A) What kind of relation between inside and outside operates in Machiavelli's text; more specifically, to what extent do rulers do things to be seen? What is the disjunction between being and seeming?

B) Why should a ruler keep his promise? Why should we keep our promises? And what kind of tally-system is involved with keeping, bending, or breaking promises?

C) Is it better to be loved or feared? Why does Machiavelli posit this pairing of terms (usually we think of love and hate, bravery and fear)? Can the question be answered as posed? If yes, respond; if no, then reformulate and have the person to your left respond.

D) Once a ruler possesses a strong city, what does he need to do to maintain it? In what ways might this correspond to things in our own lives, things over which we exercise some measure of control?

E) In the world described by Machiavelli, is it enough to be lucky or fortunate?

F) Is Machiavelli really saying "then ends justify the means?" Whose ends? What means?

G) E. M. Forster, when commenting on the laws then existing in England to imprison consenting adults for same-sex relations, said "It is better to betray the government than your friends." What is Machiavelli's view of friends? What is his view of the governing body's capacity and duty to impose laws, however arbitrary?

H) What overarching order governs the world as described by Machiavelli? What kind of justice prevails? To what extent do you judge these forces as operating in the world?

# III. Drawing the Line

The form of teaching discussed in this chapter does not involve grading. Therefore I have no statistical way of knowing whether or the extent to which the material was delivered effectively, or if the format used for the lessons was appropriate to the subject matter. I did not administer an exit survey to determine what if any of the basics had been retained, and so I will never know exactly what was learned from the courses just described. And yet, something came to my attention that is worthy of being repeated, and in doing so I will bring this chapter to a close.

A person who came to every session of "Books with Bill" told me that she took a decisive stand at work involving a peculiar case, and was not sure she would have done so prior to encountering the ideas that came out of our seminar. She judged it necessary to advise a client against doing something that she felt was at best questionable legally, but which seemed inherently wrong on the surface. If the proposal had been implemented as requested, then it was likely the public would have been allowed to make an incorrect association that would have been favorable regarding the client's "for-profit" hospital. Specifically the client wanted to name a health-care facility after a saint (religious-medical institutions are tax-exempt and have the reputation of helping those in need). The attorney pointed out that potentially it was fraud because the hospital had no right of association—religious or otherwise—with that saint. Another member of the firm, even after being advised of the relevant points of law and the potential risks and financial liabilities, thought that the client still should use the name. He argued that, essentially, it was a "dollar issue" (meaning the client—and the law firm—could put money aside in case there was an investigation leading to a fine). After all, he rationalized further, it was merely a civil statute and not a criminal one. But for one attorney at least, this was not simply a "dollar issue" nor was it as innocent as simply giving a name to a hospital. As an officer of the court she felt it was incumbent on her, and the law firm of which she was a partner, not only to advise the client of the potential risks but also strongly to counsel against using the name of a saint on the grounds that it defrauded the public. By taking a stand here, and refusing to budge on the issue, it is possible that everyone involved was spared breaking the law (as it is written) and incurring unnecessary expenses down the road. But, more importantly, what might be termed ethical behavior was demonstrated in word—and in deed.

By the end of the episode the attorney who had wanted the deal to go through at all costs (literally) recognized that he had lost sight of his moral bearings. He acknowledged that by going out of his way to do whatever the client wanted, he had ignored what, as he put it "deep-

down" he knew was "right." And so too for many of us, whether teachers or students, attorneys or health-care investors: even when the line
between right and wrong is not clearly drawn, we often know the better
course even though, at times, we choose to do otherwise and rationalize
the choice afterward. Familiarity with the lessons that are embedded in
works from the world's great literary traditions can keep us mindful of
and sensitive to what, in the broadest sense, is deemed the ethical course
of action—as at least one attorney realized, counseled others, and made
part of her dealings at work and in the world. Here then is a person who
has learned she has no more need of an ethics teacher.

# Chapter 5

## The Sword of Truth

### I. Introduction

I magine yourself at a hands-on workshop with, perhaps, art teachers, nurse practitioners, law professors, humanities lecturers, MBA program administrators, and ethics instructors. You are all armed with foam rubber swords and told to do whatever it takes to be the last person standing. Naturally you can negotiate for teams and partners along the way, as frequently happens in the workaday world. But, in the end, it must be your skill and cunning, your ability to improvise and learn as you go, that will distinguish you from the pack. Your facility at improvising—whether in fencing, in the performing arts, or in life itself—determines the extent to which you can adapt creatively and responsively to the anarchic conditions all around you so you then can reconfigure them into something that helps you realize, and move toward, your goal. The battlefield simulation starkly reveals the kinds of insights that make for lasting, lifelong, learning. After all, we are more likely to take to heart such lessons when we have discovered them for ourselves while working in tandem with others.

Imagine further how you might begin to use fencing as a metaphor for demonstrating, and for putting into practice, innovative learning and teaching. Certainly strategies for "making the point" apply in both fencing and teaching, but there is much more to consider as well. And so the goal of this chapter is to flesh out other connections, especially as pertains to some of the ways that even the most controlled approaches to making points—in fencing as in teaching—involve anarchy and rely on improvisation. Successful and graceful improvisation, though, does not just happen. It is the result of careful training and a working knowledge of what choices are available—and of coming up with options that build on these but which may not have been tried before or which may not be self-evident. This last point gets at the essence of what makes some teachers, like some fencers, more likely to connect with others and thus to let learning happen.

The battle simulation just mentioned is known by fencing instructors as "The Bouting Method" (Beguinet et al., 1999), although it usually involves just two fencers at a time. It would be recognized, in practice if not in name, by Iris Zimmermann the current world champion just as it would have been by the ancient world conqueror Alexander the Great. And while the ultimate aim of sword fighting in the West may have changed in the last 2,300 years, its fundamentals remain the same. "Even though our path is completely different from the warrior arts of the past, it is not necessary to abandon totally the old ways. Absorb venerable traditions into this new Art by clothing them with fresh garments, and build on the classic styles to create better forms" (Ueshiba, 1992: 49).

In moving from the commotion of the battlefield to the more orderly pairing off of sword-players, my goal in what follows is to distill fencing to its most basic elements so you can discern how they might easily be transferred and applied to your own areas of instruction. Accordingly (and mindful of Nietzsche's warning which brought Chapter 3 to its close) this chapter seeks to contain the potential for chaos from within by deferring to a model of traditional organization that is already at hand. This chapter, therefore, is patterned after the main aspects classical fencing: beginning with the salute, moving to the guard, and then taking into account the four types of possible activity—preparations, offensive, defensive, and counter-offensive.

From the outset though it must be understood that, as in most every area of instruction, fencing is best taught by appealing to the different senses. Thus, what has been a staple of fencing instruction for millennia, lately has become a popular pedagogical insight which has resulted in some refreshing changes in classroom instruction; namely the recognition that students learn differently and tend to fall into at least one of several main types of intelligences (Gardner, 1983). This was a point I developed in Chapter 2 in terms of four main types of learning proclivities [see again FIGURE 2.2]. Through practice, fencing instruction over the ages has acknowledged that people retain and apply lessons in different ways, each according to his or her physical make-up and intellectual predispositions. If it helps you as a teacher, you can refer to these intelligences as multiple and look to the needs of your students accordingly. Still, it is a commonplace, and has been for centuries, that fencing involves the senses of hearing, seeing, and touching, with each reinforcing the other through movement. For example, the athlete *hears* the coach's verbal descriptions of specific moves and later listens to strategies for executing those movements; she *sees* the coach demonstrate those same moves, first slowly and then at bouting speed—and also, later, she *sees* the cues and openings (as they are called) that invite specific attacks and later can analyze them through reading and writing after the physical activity stops; during the lesson she *feels* the pressure of the blade, or the absence of the blade, and thereby comes to know when and how to score the hit. From these basics, which activate all the senses (including the smell of fear and the taste of victory), everything else follows.

Whether learning the basics in the context of a teacher-workshop or with the goal of becoming a competitive fencer, the coach (or instructor) seeks to train and condition the athlete (or student) so she will be able to transfer and apply the target skills. In the case of classroom or computer-assisted instruction, for example, this might mean facilitating collaborative learning models, perhaps setting up tracks so that individuals can pursue special topics at their own pace and then share what they have learned with their peers so as to get a much larger picture than would otherwise have been possible through the more traditional lecture/listen format. In the case of fencing, more specifically, this translates into having students pair up and learn from bouting situations, and later work with—and thus teach—one another. Among fencers this is known as an "exchange drill" (Bradford, 1994: 12). It is especially effective for making the student confront the dynamic nature of the sport that unites body and mind. And so while any movement learned while standing in one place may fix it in your mind so that you can create a "body memory," still it will not recreate the reality of the dynamic rhythm of the ever-shifting distance and play of motion that you need to take into account when actually fencing. This is equally true in theatre, as it is in transplant surgery, courtroom litigation, and quantum physics.

In what follows then, by drawing on accepted pedagogical fencing methodologies as well as from case-method research, I will suggest the extent to which the fundamentals of fencing are analogous to those of other disciplines. Analogy proceeds upon the supposition that every form illustrates, in some way, a principle, a law, a truth, and that this is confirmed by an illustration of the same principle in another form (Raymond, 1909: 196). Using fencing as an analogy for classroom instruction puts the spotlight on fundamental principles that pertain to a variety of different forms of learning and areas of study. Using an analogy in this way helps bring into focus what otherwise might remain just outside your routine field of vision. My aim in doing so is to indicate how, using lessons learned from fencing, you might begin to rethink the goals and basic skills of your discipline from the ground-up and then to integrate and apply those same lessons in your own areas of teaching— no matter how traditional or how computer-driven those areas may seem.

# II. The Way of the Sword

The Bouting Method has the advantage of drawing on people's natural abilities and interests. It counters the more traditional model that seeks at the outset to correct, control, and perfect the formal aspects of swordsmanship. That approach, while historically effective in military training, has the unfortunate result of dampening the student's initial enthusiasm for the activity by causing her to feel overwhelmed by all there is to learn. This is one reason why the Bouting Method enjoys popularity among teachers today, no matter where or when they originally learned to fence and to coach. Using it allows students to see for themselves, almost at once, that fencing is far from the swash-buckling, rapier-waving free-for-all depicted in movies. By virtue of reflecting on their initial "jump into the fray" efforts, students quickly recognize that point-control and minimal blade-work (indeed, the conservation of movement in whatever way possible), is the key to success in fencing. A coach can tell this to beginning fencers over and over again, but until the student experiences it for himself, he is doomed to harbor the misconception that throwing himself at the other player will get his point to the target. At first sheer force and power may work, but eventually the attacker will grow weary and the defender then can overcome him easily through subtle movements and slight variations in her position. "Even the most powerful person has a limited sphere of strength; draw him outside of that sphere and into your own, and his strength will dissipate" (Ueshiba, 1992: 101).

The Bouting Method works well because most people, innately, like to try things on their own, whether or not they have been shown the proper technique. In this regard, think, for example, of children with chalk at a wall or day-traders at a computer terminal. You can't keep them from striking out on their own no matter how messy the outcome of their efforts. The effective coach anticipates and works with this natural impulse to see for oneself what will happen, come-what-may. This being understood, the coach will then set up situations in which the student *intrinsically* can acknowledge that she is ready for instruction. In so doing, she learns for herself how to frame the right kinds of questions to draw appropriate answers—the answers to things she thinks she needs to know. Trial and error along these lines thus puts the student in the right frame of mind for isolating the kinds of instruction that she is ready to receive. This is the key to affective learning and the cue for effective teaching.

Coaches—teachers—who want to apply the Bouting Method should keep in mind that even though it may cause a great deal of "sound and fury signifying nothing," it is far from a random approach. In fact, in it we can see at work the four main components used in most every method that seeks to impart basic skills, fencing included: *demonstrating, teaching, fixating, perfecting.* I have put these terms in italics because, like many points made in this chapter, they come right out of the Coaching Manual compiled by the United States Fencing Association (Beguinet et al., 1999).

More specifically, in the Bouting Method students are given equipment, a few ground rules and safety tips, and then told to go at it. After a fair amount of confusion, they will stop to ask how to defend incoming attacks and then ask about strategies for attacking. It has been my experience that students are always concerned initially with keeping from getting hit; that is, with not being caught unprepared or unaware and thus looking bad in front of their peers. (Not surprisingly, this characterizes students in Freshman English no less than those in graduate seminars on Aesthetics.) In this the students show they are ready to begin learning. The coach will intervene to answer general questions as briefly as possible so he can turn them loose again to try out what they were just told. The next time the student stops to ask a question, it will be more specific. She will, most likely, isolate a situation and show what she sees as her possible options in that case; then she will ask very direct questions about when and how the resulting movements should be done. The coach will be asked to show her, to *demonstrate*, the move. This becomes the alert coach's cue that the student is ready for further *teaching*. He can identify sets of specific drills that are geared to help the student with what she has determined she needs or wants to know. Then the moves, or skills, can be *fixated* by precise execution, many repetitions under easy and unchanging situations (a time-tried approach, especially well known to participants of the United States Fencing Association's "Coaches College," which is referred to the Blocked Method). When the coach judges that the students is ready to put it all together, to *perfect* the skills, he will change the speed, timing, and rhythm, thus simulating bouting conditions. The coach then can add two or more similar strokes that might arise in bouts (known as the Serial Method). Building on this, the student can begin to transfer knowledge regarding one skill to other, similar movements. She is ready at last to fence (Random Method).

Getting the student to move from simulated conditions to the real thing as soon as she is ready to do so with some proficiency will help her to develop her own style and to feel as though she has made the learning a part of herself. "Instructors can impart only a fraction of the teaching. It is through your own devoted practice that the mysteries of the Art are brought to life" (Ueshiba, 1992: 58). So while the teaching of basic skills may be broken down into the familiar stages of *demonstrating, teaching, fixating,* and *perfecting*, obviously there is more to fencing, to any discipline, than this. It needs to be done on the move; and the skills need, quite literally, to be put to the test.

Learning involves more than memorizing things that one can reproduce when called on or given the appropriate cue to do so. Some sort of transference of basic facts and a translation of them into some other form or medium must take place along the way for learning to be said to have occurred. At some point wider applications of the material, often culminating in something new, must come into play or else what has been learned is but a collection of so many disconnected, though perhaps noteworthy, facts and moves and definitions. This applies in fencing as in other disciplines, whether mathematics or law or French. And so too each discipline has a history—a history that is both unique and also which is tied in with other intellectual developments and cultural movements in the West. In this respect, the history of the sword is bound up with the history of humanity; and we might even say that the history of the sword (at least up to the 20th century) *is* the history of humanity (Burton, 1884: xv).

Like every major discipline, fencing has a history of how it has been taught in different lands and at different times (Garret, 1994: 2). Over the years and in different climes, rival schools have developed, each touting its method as being superior to others. Obviously if a leader of one school of thought promotes his program over others, then his method (and the resulting articles and books) will be embraced and practiced by many working in the field; and thus, for good or ill, it will become a benchmark. But the method, or program, or "learning concept" that wins out and becomes institutionalized need not necessarily be the one that is actually the most effective for acquiring the designated target skills. Despite debates over which approach is preferable, the basic skills are never really contested. What is argued about though includes: how those skills are to be taught, the order in which they should be learned, who should learn them and under what conditions, at what stage they should be introduced, and how best they can be reinforced and assessed and measured. . . .

Irrespective of which of these concerns gets voiced most vociferously though, rarely, if ever, are the fundamentals at issue. For example, "whole language" advocates, like their detractors, all agree that recognizing letters is important to the reading process. So too in contemporary literary studies, whether or not one is adamant that historically under-represented figures should be taught in the context of basic college courses, no one seriously would claim that "great figures" (like Dante, Shakespeare, Goethe) are not worthy of being taught. By the same token, whatever else we may think about Columbus's motives for exploration or about the emerging slave trade, no reasonably informed middle-school curriculum designer or principal would suggest that the Spanish presence in America should be skipped or whitewashed.

In acknowledging the tradition—and, as we saw in Chapter 3, at times repeating it—we are not necessarily kowtowing to it. In acknowledging the tradition we are recognizing its place in an on-going cultural discourse of which we are a vital part and to which we are contributing members. In fact, to be effective teachers and affective learners, we must seek to acknowledge our place in the stream of contributions and, to some extent, show our familiarity with it. We need to do this before we can do anything of lasting merit in our profession; and, in so doing, we demonstrate through our actions the extent to which we respect and take seriously our chosen fields of endeavor and areas of instruction.

And this leads into the first thing any student of fencing is taught: the salute.

## 1. Salute

With your mask off, you always begin by saluting the other person—whether it is the coach, another player, or even perhaps the audience before whom you are demonstrating proper technique. Like the gesture of bowing in Aikido or touching gloves in boxing, the salute is designed to call to mind that sportsmanship should prevail from beginning to end.

The salute is a gesture toward the other player in a non-combative way that reminds both athletes it is a game into which they are about to enter. Indeed, as Johan Huizinga goes on to explain, among the characteristics of play are: that it is free (is, in fact, freedom); it is a stepping out of real life into a temporary sphere of activity with a disposition all of its own; and it is distinct from ordinary life both as to locality and duration—it contains its own course and meaning. "To dare, to take risks, to bear uncertainty, to endure tension—these are the essence of the play spirit. Tension adds to the importance of the game and, as it increases, enables the player to forget that he is only playing" (Huizinga, 1955: 51). This understanding of the power of the contest, of the play, to overtake and utterly preoccupy the players in fencing (as in theatre and as in the classroom) gives added weight to the importance of the salute.

The salute in fencing pays tribute to the tacit agreement both players have with respect to the sport in general, to that contest in particular, and to the tradition that stretches out before and after them—a tradition of which they are a vital, if temporary, part. We must recall that not long ago swearing by a sword was the highest form of an oath; just as surrendering one's sword symbolized utter submission, and having one's sword ceremonially broken was the ultimate in social degradation (Burton, 1884: xv).

The salute at the beginning and at the end (followed by a shaking of the non-weapon hands), reminds each player of his responsibility to himself, to the sport and to its history, and to the other player. The goal, of course, is not to injure one another, and every precaution is taken to make sure this doesn't happen. The salute, then, keeps alive the sense of seriousness of purpose and honorable intent that stands at the origins of swordsmanship—as an ancient art as well as a modern sport. The salute reminds us of the heritage of fencing, and of the solemn duty that we have to it in our roles as people who have made a conscious decision to continue the art in its current form. Only when play is a recognized cultural function is it bound up with notions of obligation and duty (Huizinga, 1955: 8).

I would mention here that competitive fencing today is now organized so that people of similar ages, genders, and special abilities are allowed to compete with like contestants. A ten-year old just starting out is not likely to learn much (or have much fun) by being beaten by someone twice her age and size. By the same token, as a person who has been at the sport for over thirty years, while I enjoy playing against athletic college students (and occasionally being beaten soundly by them), it is in some ways more satisfying for me to compete against athletes who have similar tactical experiences and who have a back-log of competition strategies and "war-stories." As another veteran put it: "The fun is in the game itself, just as it always was. The challenge of an opponent and his abilities, the strategy, tactics, psychology, execution of technique . . . that's all there. It just doesn't take place as rapidly as it used to" (Micahnik, 2001: 10). But whether in a training session, at a veterans' meet, or competing in a world youth tournament, fencers, whatever their status or classification, always salute one another before and after a drill, bout, or contest.

## 2. On Guard

As in all disciplines, in fencing there is a point of departure that is also a point to which you return time and again. This is not so much a comfort zone, like that spot of safety many instructors search for in their teaching and, once they find it, seldom venture from it (as was discussed in the Introduction). The guard is that unique position, correct for each fencer, that permits her to be equally ready for offense, defense, counter offense—basically, to be balanced and open for any movement, whether of the feet or hands or body (Garret, 1994: 27). One is ready to move—or to remain stationary; she is content, and prepared and able, to do whatever the situation requires. One must be sufficiently trained and self-possessed to have the patience to wait and to know when to initiate movement. You must learn to be secure with what you know and where you are, and to act on it accordingly. "The key to good technique is to keep your hands, feet, and hips straight and centered. If you are centered, you can move freely" (Ueshiba, 1992: 69). Likewise: "A good

stance and posture reflect a proper state of mind" (Ueshiba, 1992: 68).
To be sure though, bluff and bravado can play a big part in one's proper
stance. Some fencers feel it gives them a slight edge even before the bout
begins. Any advantage to which you can lay claim, so much the better—
and this applies as well to our teaching. Knowing when to act or not to
act in a given situation, like knowing when to back off from a question
(whether because of the requirements of your syllabus or simply owing
to common sense), and like knowing when and how to respond to a
request from a department chair or dean—all of these things come back
to being "on guard." This leads then into how we go about arming ourselves in advance of getting involved with the techniques and specific
tactics of our trades: preparations.

## 3. Preparations

Whether getting lectures ready or ordering books and supplies, whether
organizing last year's research notes and grant applications to make way
for this year's, each of us must coordinate materials and resources (including our time) if we hope to meet the challenges that inevitably come
our way, and to do so with some degree of success and professionalism.
Some people require more time for their courses to come together, to
ferment as it were, even after having selected (or been assigned) the
material to be covered. Such people, therefore, might need to start the
whole processes months in advance so as to have time to reflect on the
material and thus to be open to whatever the books and prospective topics have to disclose about the core and content of one's course of instruction.

And yet irrespective of how much lead-time one has—and all too
often, especially in the cases of adjuncts, part-timers, and graduate students, the TBA (teacher to be announced) is slotted into a class or section the very week that formal instruction begins—one can only be prepared so far. There are always unforeseen circumstances that undermine
even the best of intentions and planning efforts. In the face of this, some
teachers over-prepare and, ironically, as a result, run the risk of not
reaching their target goals. It is a common problem among even the
"best teachers" to have too much material for the time allowed; or, to
have so grand a thesis or theme that one's students will have difficulty
following the lofty drift of the lesson. Improvising freely and creatively
(along the lines mentioned in the opening paragraph of this chapter), so

as to make the best of such situations, is what distinguishes the seasoned, and often lucky, teacher from the rigid, though often well-intentioned, lecturer. This applies to the teaching of fencing as well as to the student's repetition and execution of specific moves.

Preparations are basically of two types, body movements and blade actions. Seeing them in this way, represented schematically [FIGURE 5.1], takes some of the fear out of there being seemingly infinite, apparently anarchic, combinations of moves from which to choose. Although we may see our choices presented neatly at a glance, this does not necessarily allay our fear that we are choosing correctly from among the possible alternatives. Habit inadvertently may dictate what we end up doing, for old habits are hard to shake [see again, FIGURE 0.1]. Some choices will always be better than others given the circumstances, but learning to distinguish from among these will come only in time and with practice and patience—and through trial and error; through improvisation. This is another place where education and anarchy dance hand in hand if true and lasting learning is destined to take place.

## Body Movements

Mobility is essential to making a point. The fencer needs to get her body in the right place at the right time to do whatever move is called for in the situation, whether advancing, lunging, retreating. . . . So too in classroom instruction, the student literally has to get herself to class with all of the required supplies and assignments. The teacher, like the coach, has the task of demanding that the student respect the distance precisely. This applies not only to the roles each has taken on, but also how to position herself with respect to where the teacher is going—in fencing, literally up and down the fencing strip; in the classroom, figuratively with respect to the drift of the lesson. The material being conveyed always is, or should be, just within reach of the student (it is counterproductive to learning when the teacher constantly moves out of reach just as the student is about "get it"). In usual drilling situations, it is the student's job quite literally to get herself to the target—whether by virtue of bodily movements using the feet, trunk, arm, or fingers; or by virtue of blade work; or a combination of body and blade movements. In the end though, it is up to the student to do whatever she judges is required to keep pace with the teacher and, in the end, to get the point. The same applies to the classroom teacher with respect to his specific *instructional*

**Figure 5.1**

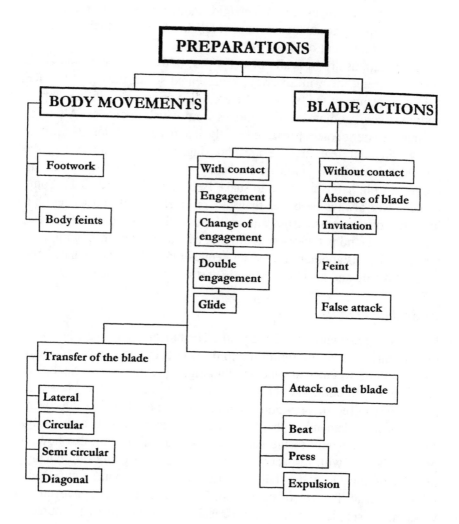

*objectives* [Mager, 1975: 7], just as it does to the coach. For once the target has been identified, one's capacity to move toward it—or better still creating situations so that the target comes to you—is what makes for the successful realization of one's plan of action, whether for student or teacher, for athlete or coach.

In fencing, if your body is out of place from where it needs to be, then either you will fall short of the mark and look bad for having misjudged where you should have ended up; or you will hit off target and look sloppy for having lacked proper point control; or you (or your point) will go past the other player's target area and you will look as vulnerable as you are in this situation. The analogy holds for the basics in making a point in academic work as well: the ability to think logically, appropriately, and creatively and to write cogently, aptly, and descriptively will distinguish you as a person who judges well the nature of his topic or theme and acts artfully on the perceived relation of a specific form to the material at hand. In fencing, while a creative response to familiar moves is at times successful because unexpected, more often than not a traditional move, when properly executed, remains the most effective and efficient thing one can do. This is not simply repetition because every situation is slightly different, especially given the variables with respect to movement and timing.

But basic communication skills, and the study of rhetoric and logic, are hardly the only areas of intellectual endeavor where points need to be made efficiently and elegantly. Mathematics, for example, immediately comes to mind, as does medicine and law, as well as the fruits of political economics. In all of these domains, as in fencing, clear and decisive thinking, though not necessarily the most rapid actions, often will make for swift and enduring success. Initiating actions in a timely, though not necessarily reactive, way provides better results than does reacting haphazardly or belatedly as a result of succumbing to habit and, to some extent, fear.

To trace out the analogy now with respect to body movements in fencing [FIGURE 5.1, left branch]: clear thinking in general corresponds to *footwork* (how the body is brought into position and toward the target for the decisive stroke to be made); well-thought out propositions, subtle arguments, and theories based on solid empirical data correspond to *body feints*. The first involves how you carry yourself; the second, your body language and, overall, how you comport yourself. In concert with body movements are blade actions, which correspond to your various technical methods and tactical options.

## *Blade Actions*

While the rules of fencing foil and épée require that you hit only with the point to score a touch, those of sabre allow for cuts as well. In all events though, no matter what weapon is used, the blade alone stands between you and the other player. As words are to language and communication, so blades carry intentions and meanings. Also, as will be discussed in my concluding remarks, the teacher speaks most effectively to his students not in words alone but through the blade as well. The teacher speaks with his blade.

Working our way through the possible options [FIGURE 5.1, right branch], blade actions come about in two ways really: with contact and without contact, whether or not you initiate it. Without contact involves creating an expectation that your blade will be in one place when in fact it will be in another by the time the other player seeks it. So too these principles of presenting by non-presenting can help in your teaching. This is not intended as a conundrum, but as a very practical application of an option available to the teacher and coach, as well as to the student and athlete during practical applications of lessons undertaken. While I am treating it here as a tactical choice, it can be considered as part of a metaphysical program as well if you like: "Cast off limiting thoughts and return to true emptiness. Stand in the midst of the Great Void. This is the secret of the Way of a Warrior" (Ueshiba, 1992: 110).

One of the main tactical principles of fencing, particularly in foil and sabre, is known as "absence of blade." In such a case, no blade is threatening the student; there is no *apparent* threat. This is analogous in the classroom to letting the student ask the questions and thereby direct the discussion of the material, when you (the teacher) know most of the places this might be leading. Thus, such an invitation to get the student to make the first move, in fencing, is the deliberate showing of an opening or a cue to get her to do something immediate and decisive, *as the opening is being creating* rather than after it has been executed. In the classroom we might ask students to follow what they take to be a direct way into the subject and then when they think they are about to get it, to shift lines so as to open up the analysis to the next level. They will have made the leap with you if they have in fact understood the principles that came before. If you truly understand a certain principle in its entirety, you can put it into practice at will. And so too with the feint: you start and let the other go for it, only to realize that she needs to change to another tactic because she has missed something. Your feint has drawn her in and now she must improvise accordingly. The false attack from fencing is most familiar to classroom teachers as the proverbial "straw man," a case that is easy to overcome—if the student can recognize it as such, get to it in time, and dismantle it in the right sequence.

There are many more ways of proceeding once contact has been made, whether on the fencing strip or in the classroom. Engagement of the blade is simply to move into proximity of the other: in fencing, her blade; in the classroom, something she holds, metaphorically, like an opinion or point of view. To engage the blade, like engaging the student's interest, is to pose something quite direct to which she needs to respond. Change of engagement would correspond to shifting from one side of the blade to the other; analogously, an abrupt shift in the line of inquiry while still keeping contact with the student's point. Shoring up your view on a case that is being discussed in the classroom corresponds in fencing to the double engagement (and, building on this, the change of double engagement would be the execution of two changes of engagement in immediate succession). The glide in fencing is the preparation of an attack consisting of constant contact, sliding along the opponent's blade. This technique can be transferred to classroom teaching as well: setting up a discussion or making a point by following closely at every step of the way work that students have already presented and then, without pressuring them, having them see what will result if you follow it to its logical conclusion.

And there are attacks on the blade by way of preparing to make the hit: the beat, press, and expulsion [FIGURE 5.1, bottom right]. These motions all make decisive contact on the blade at just the right place or else they will fail. If this happens (say, if the other fencer retreats, or slightly moves his blade out of the way), then you should not continue the action but be ready for anything that might be thrown at you now that you are no longer in control of the rhythm. The beat in fencing correlates to striking at what the other puts before you, whether it is an idea, proposition, business plan, or what-have-you. The press is something the teacher might do to get a gentle reaction from the student that he can then use to further the line of inquiry. The expulsion in fencing is sharp, powerful, prolonged pressure put on the blade, executed by sliding toward the strong part of the other's blade, which sends it flying out of her hand. In the classroom this might play out in terms of keeping steady pressure on the point being discussed until you have gotten to the root issue so that the student no longer can maintain a false presupposition or ungrounded opinion and must release it, acknowledging it to be, well, untenable.

Once these simple preparatory blade actions are understood we can build on them in ways that seem to have more flourish; namely, as transfers of the blade [FIGURE 5.1, bottom left]. Here the coach teaches the student to engage and seize the opponent's blade and progressively to control it until completion of the action, which will result in scoring a touch. The four ways of doing this are lateral (staying in the same line), circular (leading, without losing contact, away from and then into the same line where you started), semi-circular (from high to low or vice versa), and diagonal (from high to the opposite low line or vice versa). In the classroom the lateral transfer might correspond to using homologies or isomorphisms; circular, using tautologies or paradoxes; semi-circular, moving from well applied hyperbole (overstatement) to bathos (understatement) or vice versa; diagonal, cutting across disciplines.

Each of these processes involves thinking about where you want to end up and where you anticipate the student will be by the end of the lesson. As with any instructional objective the teacher must know and be able to state quite specifically what he or she wants the student to be able to *do*, under what conditions, and what counts as acceptable performance—to repeat the time-tried triad of *performance, conditions,* and *criterion* (Mager, 1975: 21). In fencing, as in the classroom, knowledge of probable outcomes is paramount, especially when seeking to execute transfers—whether of the blade from one place to another, or of ideas from one discipline to another. In either case the outcome of a well-executed and memorable transfer tends to delight and to inspire wonder; further, it is hoped, perhaps even to incite and instigate lasting learning. Thus continuous contact and progressive monitoring (in fencing, control of the blade) is required or else the desired transfer will not have the desired effect. But this contact (or control) need not be a mania; simply a given. Only in this way, and through training and discipline, can the teacher—like the student—demonstrate proper preparations for the matter at hand: making valid points and doing so with verve.

## 4. Offensive

The terms that have come down to us when speaking about fencing tactics are adversarial. But this should come as no surprise given the character of many and most of our cultural institutions. Perhaps owing to the way we contextualized confrontation in terms of a contest, we think little today of the "versus" that stands between two parties in a law-suit or between the accused and the State in our courts of law, any more than we remark on metaphors of warfare regularly used in business and politics. When running for political office, for example, no matter how worthy your opponent may be, she is still running *against* you. To speak of attacks, then, is natural when it comes to planning strategy in whatever the domain. And yet not every plan is designed to *overcome* your opponent. At times it is enough to win someone over.

The object of fencing, when all is said and done, is to defeat your opponent by making more points aginst him than he makes on you while following the rules of that particular weapon and contest, and all the while seeking to honor the sport (as was discussed with respect to the salute). Can the same be said for teaching in general? Or is this the place where our analogy between fencing and teaching breaks down? For teachers do not seek to defeat students. And yet, might it not be the case that even though most teachers are devoted to imparting lessons and care about their teaching, it is just not possible for them to have every student's best interest in mind?

As was suggested in the Introduction regarding what makes a teacher a teacher, no single answer to the question can ever give a full and accurate account of the range of possibilities. Still, as was intimated in the Credo of Chapter Two, certain things do seem to remain constant about the ethical obligations teachers have toward their students—a point that was fleshed out in Chapter 4. Practice bears out that the actual range of possibilities for appropriate and responsible action however, whether in classroom teaching or in fencing, is not as vast as might at first be imagined (or feared). So while there may be seemingly infinite variables opened up from within these several options, as Chapter 1 made clear, there are ways of contracting and circumscribing the chaos of chance and change into manageable and memorable curricular activities. Chapter 3 pointed out further that what might seem like repetition often is the first step toward genuine innovation. With this in mind, Chapter 5 seeks to reach back into what has gone before it, and to weave the even-chapters (including the Introduction) with the odd-numbered ones, thus providing a further twist to our questioning of what makes a teacher a teacher. In doing so I would set up the conclusion of this chapter by wrapping up the gist of the offensive moves, and then pass on the defensive and counter-offensive options in fencing—mirrored in teaching.

There are only three ways to make a point. Offensive actions (with or without preparatory body movements or blade actions), as can be seen at a glance [FIGURE 5.2], are of three kinds: attacks, ripostes, and varied offensive moves. That is all; there is nothing more.

## Attacks

Attacks follow more or less the same pattern as those main actions discussed in the previous section. And it is here that we uncover the essence of fencing: whatever else may accompany the attack, before or after, there are really only three ways to score a touch (not counting penalty situations). First, you can go in straight; second, you can go in under (the bell) or; third, you can go in over (the tip). These three forms of attack make up the sum total of the physical technique of fencing; all the rest is tactics. To put it more metaphysically: "Ultimately you must forget about technique. The further you progress, the fewer teachings there are. The Great Path is really No Path" (Ueshiba, 1992: 114).

But, to bring it back to practical applications in the classroom: either you approach the material directly (straight); or you start low, with the rudiments, and come around (disengage); or else you pitch it in over the top to goad students to reach for it (cut over). To illustrate just the disengage, in philosophy you might start with the origins of certain words (like "being"); or, in anatomy, you might start with the Latin designations for body parts and then build up to an understanding of how these names identify a location or perhaps the connective state of those muscles or bones or organs. In fencing the three main ways to make the point can be reinforced by actions on the blade, whether transfers or attacks, like those already discussed. Branching off the simple attacks are any number of ramifications, known as compound attacks; which is to say offensive actions preceded by one or more feints or actions on the blade. Still though, when all is said and done, if you are going to make a point, you need to go in straight, to go in under (the bell), or to go in over (the tip).

## Ripostes

The riposte is an offensive action executed after a parry. (The parry is simply a defensive blade movement that blocks the opponent's offensive action. I will have more to say about this in the upcoming section on

Figure 5.2

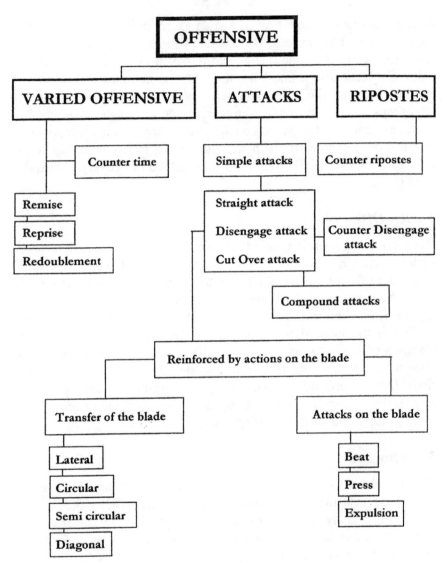

parries, understood more properly as an aspect of defense.) It may be either simple or compound. Basically ripostes are direct (which is to say, executed in the same line as that in which the parry occurred) or indirect (executed in a line other than the one in which the parry occurred); and sometimes they can be delayed (executed after a pause). Off of these possibilities comes the counter riposte, which is executed by one or more feints or by actions on the blade. I urge you to exercise your imagination and come up with ways that these tactics might apply to your own intellectual discipline, favored method of delivery, and style of teaching.

## *Varied Offensive*

Other effective offensive moves involve counter time (an action made against a counter offensive action), the remise (simple direct offensive or counter offensive action made after the offensive or counter offensive action has been parried but when your riposte is delayed or absent), reprise (simple *in*direct, *compound* offensive or counter offensive action made after the initial offensive or counter offensive is parried, when the riposte is delayed or absent), and redoublement (a forward conformation often with new footwork after an initial offensive action is short or parried). It has been said that the remise is the result of calculation; the reboublement from inspiration (Gaugler, 1997: 49). So too in our classroom lectures and when executing our lesson plans. . . .

## 5. Defensive

Now that the student has been instructed in how to hit the other player, she needs to consider how to keep from getting hit [FIGURE 5.3]. Some of this will already be familiar to her by instinct, but the proper execution of defensive moves is paramount to developing the skills for fencing. The best defense seemingly is the one that requires the least amount of effort and energy. Again, the principle of conservation of movement needs to be kept in mind.

## *Evasions*

Moving your body out of the way of the oncoming blade is one approach to defense. Of the many options for accomplishing this, the most basic is simply to step back; and while there are many ways to do so, the main

**Figure 5.3**

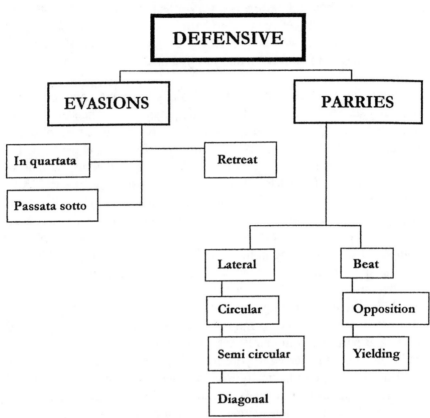

term fencers use for it is "retreat." In the classroom, this might correspond to letting the students work collaboratively on writing a response to a case, solving a problem, or getting the answers to a work-sheet or lab project. Here the teacher steps back, as it were, and observes the relative success of the groups as they grapple with issues—whether in terms of content or method, or both—that have been covered in the course of previous instruction. This also gives the teacher a chance to see which students emerge as the true leaders, whether vocal or otherwise. Brought together by a shared challenge, students can learn from one another by trial and error and get at the heart of the matter in a common language that may not be the way it was taught in class. So too in fencing: nothing teaches distance and timing better than working in pairs; just advancing and retreating, keeping distance with the designated leader and then switching roles. In a bout the retreat is a very effective way to defend against the attack because it gets you out of harm's way and, while maintaining a good guard, gives you a split second to get in position for the next move you intend to initiate. In this way you take control of the rhythm of the bout.

Sometimes the best way to further things in your favor is to step back and survey the situation from a safe perspective. The same applies to one's teaching. Reflection is essential for true advancement of learning and improvement in quality of instruction. Evasions however do not require that you always step back, but also step either to the side or slightly forward [FIGURE 5.3, left]. You can defend against attacks by displacing your body, like the *in quartata*—a quarter turning of the body with your guard in a position known as "4th opposition." Or you can use the sonorous *passata sotto*, a counter attack against both simple and compound attacks ending in the outside high line (Gaugler, 1997: 47).

Italian terms like these were so commonplace in English by the time of Shakespeare that it is with a call for a *passado*, or sprightly lunge, that Mercutio incites the fight in *Romeo and Juliet* that leads to his death, and which leads Romeo to fight and kill Tybalt. This move plays an important part in this drama no less than in the history of fencing—just as it can when transferred to your teaching, metaphorically speaking. If we learn nothing else tactically from Merucutio's demise, let us at least take away with us that the pedagogical equivalent of the *passado* should be saved for just the right moment and mark a cunning culmination of what has come before it. You can score with a sprightly lunge only if you keep your point moving toward the target even as you decrease the distance between you and other player. To leap forward in fencing without heed to your point (or hers), is certain death; to do so in teaching is sheer folly.

## *Parries*

In the Renaissance a parry was defied quite practically as "the action of turning away, from one's body, the hostile steel" (Gaugler, 1997: 46). The term "parry" has crept into everyday English to mean an evasion usually by an adroit answer. It has the sense now of a comeback that puts someone in his place. Parries show that you can hold your own and stay your ground. This is true in fencing as well, for (as we have seen above) a parry is the defensive blade movement that blocks the opponent's offensive action [FIGURE 5.3, right].

There are many types of parries designed to protect specific parts of your body. For the purposes of this chapter we will not treat them all in particular, but think of them generally as a blade movement that stops the opponent's offensive action. And in the classroom too, there are plenty of occasions for defensive movements. (I am referring here to commonplace instructional methods, but I am aware that more and more some educational settings today require that teachers know how to defend themselves and to protect their students from physical harm). For example, the beat parry would be to deflect a weak argument decisively and sharply. The opposition parry would be to foreclose the possibility of an erroneous argument. The yielding parry corresponds to turning the idea or argument back on him so that what he considers to be the greatest strength of his on-coming point is what ends up making *your* point.

It cannot be overlooked that point of view generally speaking can be compared to making a point, or scoring, in fencing. Getting the point during a lecture means that the student "gets it." Likewise in fencing, to get a point means that you have successfully found a way to score a hit. Point of view involves seeing something in a certain way; and, in fencing, there are different ways to look at a series of moves. In foil and sabre for example, one man's beat is another man's parry—depending on how the judge *sees* and calls the syntax of the exchange of blades. Getting the point can depend on more than the proper and timely execution of an intended move. In some situations, you must convince the director, who oversees the contest, that your attack had priority over the other player's move—whether or not this is objectively true.

Such an understanding of point of view has little practical relevance and tactical application in épée, as there is no priority of attack (two players can score hits on one another simultaneously, a modern adaptation of the weapon's history as the traditional dueling weapon). Correspondingly this is the case in those academic areas of inquiry in which multiple, equally valid, points of view are entertained and allowed. Still point of view, as an extension of one's will more than of objective scientific inquiry, gets played out in all manner of swordplay when it comes to believing you can hit the other player before she can hit you, no matter who drew first. And this leads us to the counter offense. "The urge to be first has as many forms of expression as society offers opportunities for it. The ways in which men compete for superiority are as various as the prizes at stake. . . . But in whatever shape it comes it is always play, and it is from this point of view that we have to interpret its cultural function" (Huizinga, 1955: 105).

## 6. Counter Offensive

There are four main categories of counter offensive actions: the stop, derobement, remise, and reprise [FIGURE 5.4]. To use fencing as a springboard for transferring these moves in general education, we could say that the stop corresponds to anticipating what is about to come at you and getting your point in before the other person. The derobement (or disengagement in time employed in opposition to actions made on the blade) corresponds to an evasion of the other's attempt to take, or attack, one's thesis. This is not to give the impression that only debating techniques or rhetorical strategies are those that follow from using fencing as an analogy where counter offensive actions are concerned. For example, the remise, as we have seen (one of the varied offensive actions), is simply a replacement: the putting of the point in the place where initially it was going but never quite made contact with the target. A remise might correspond to a follow up lesson to a lab, designed to reinforce the trajectory of the unit's final objective. The reprise is a coming back to the original theme but taking it up in another way in order to reach the target; it is a renewing of the attack, often with great vigor and accompanied by surprise. In the classroom such a lesson achieved in this way would remain lodged in the memories of students for a long time to come. What they do with it from there is up to them. . . .

# III. Lessons Learned from Fencing

We stand to learn a great deal about teaching from fencing, especially if we are willing to reflect on our training even as we strive to be liberated from it. By the same token, we stand to learn a lot about our calling if we are willing to repeat and yet seek to twist free from the tradition even as we push ourselves toward our destiny. This is what I had in mind when I quoted Bakunin (*"The power to think* and *the desire to* rebel."), which now takes on added significance in the light of what has been discussed up to this point in the book. Approaching teaching in this way is tantamount to finding ways of keeping at bay, if not discovering how to allow, the New Cerberus to help you to realize your destiny [FIGURE

**Figure 5.4**

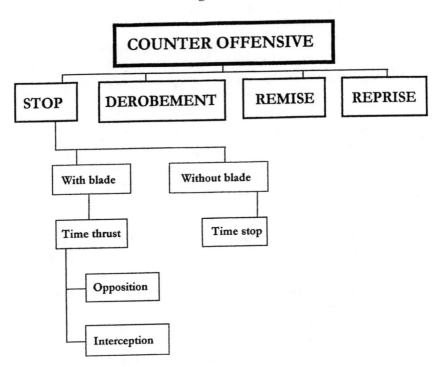

0.1]. This brings us closer still toward explaining how we can contrive (to recall words of Kropotkin at the end of the epigraph page) to satisfy our intellectual and artistic needs. For in so doing we are able to reflect and act on what is done in the classroom more boldly and creatively— and also perhaps, as Bakunin would have it, more thoughtfully and re- belliously. Such an approach however, as fencing shows us so well—and as the lines from Arnold on the epigraph page declare without equivoca- tion—, "must proceed by due course of law."

To continue this line of reflection, let us consider that fencing coaches teach day in and day out with sword in hand. What do you use? What tool, what extension of yourself and of your prior learning and training, habitually do you use most in your daily instruction? Your voice? Books? Chalk? A computer screen? With what in hand do you typically further your lessons? What is it that you rely on most regularly to convey and deliver lessons to your students, to your athletes? Into what routine have you perhaps inadvertently fallen?

These kinds of questions are germane to the task at hand and help us revive the analogy between fencing and teaching in general. Fencing, like effective classroom instruction, can cut across language barriers. Proper fencing instruction is a kind of non-verbal Esperanto. As the old adage put it: "the master talks with his blade." When a student has a question, the answer comes swiftly through practical action, for only what works successfully in the field really matters. As in business, for example, hypothetical cases may be interesting to debate on one's own time, but what counts finally is what happens in the marketplace on a given day and under whatever conditions happen to prevail. So it is in fencing. The history of dueling, with its insistence on fighting to stay alive and preserve honor, led to some remarkable developments in the "Art of Defence" that remain nascent in nearly every aspect of fencing as it is taught today.

As I intimated earlier, the adversarial terminology used in fencing, as in law and commerce, may need to be rethought so as to come up with less belligerent connotations—but only if there is a chance those implications might cease practically to apply. This does not seem very likely though as they are deeply entrenched in our language, as they are in our cultural orientation toward oppositional structures of thought and action. Semantics alone cannot dislodge them. Actions, not words, along the lines of how the fencing teacher teaches with his blade, may be called for if we are to face up to the revolution in education that is upon us (again, where revolution is understood as a recurring and natural process, like that mentioned in the Introduction, and exemplified in Chapter 1). In so doing we come closer in our own work, and in our own fields of endeavor, to accomplishing what Kropotkin boldly proposed could happen for humanity in general: to satisfy the intellectual and artistic needs of all our students at whatever their stage of schooling or education [FIGURE 4.1 and FIGURE 4.2].

Implicitly acknowledging the revolution already underway, the White House Millennium Council for the Modern Languages Association of America asked its constituent members to characterize major shifts in teaching philosophy that have occurred during the last century and to speculate on what lies ahead. Among the two hundred responses recently published, one in particular echoes my claim introduced in Chapter 1 and with which I would conclude Chapter 5: "No longer an authority figure who stands imposingly in the front of the classroom raining drops of knowledge on student sponges diligently soaking in thoughts that are memorized, reproduced, and forgotten, the teacher is now a facilitator of learning among a community of learners. Students work in groups, solve problems, speak for themselves, and teach other students" (Engar, 2000: 2000-2001). In line with this, I would have us consider further how we go about conceptualizing and discharging our duties as teachers, as well as how we devise and implement our methods of delivery and assessment, because these things determine fundamentally how we define and play out our roles as educators. It may be useful to entertain other terms that might help us get at the essence of what we think we are doing when we cast ourselves in those roles.

Old-world authoritarian terms like master and pupil have given way in modern fencing to coach and athlete. Forms of the Latin *magister* (whence are derived master, maître, and maestro) still persist in some circles, as do old-world titles in academics like Master of Arts or Business. And yet these forms of address, in America at least, often are dropped. What falls away with these titles, really though? Isn't a professor's power over the student—especially where assignments and grades are concerned—just as omnipresent whether you call her Professor Lastname or by her first name? The prevailing system remains in tact no matter what labels are used; for, as Kropotkin theorized in economic terms but which apply to the case I have introduced as well: capital will conceal itself, and yet production cannot continue to go on as it does (Kropotkin, 1886-1907/1988: 58). It is not so much production and the resulting work products that we, as teachers, need to take as the focus of our endeavors, even though this is what tends to be valued (as was argued in Chapter 3). Rather, to paraphrase Kropotkin again using his political argument to make one about the revolution in teaching that is upon us: unless we are prepared openly and avowedly to profess that the satisfaction and the needs of each individual must be our very first aim; unless we have prepared public opinion to establish itself firmly at this standpoint, the people in their next attempt to free themselves will once more suffer a defeat (Kropotkin, 1886-1907/1988: 60). This will be stated more decisively still in the Conclusion to this book just a few pages away.

What title we use, finally, matters little (if at all) unless and until we put the needs of our students first. One way of moving along this path though is to rethink what underlies our assumption of such titles and how we came to earn the right to use them. Further, we need to take into account the probable consequences of our taking them on, and carefully consider their limitations and liberties. It may be the case that our whole attitude with respect to instruction could begin to shift toward more innovative and expressive modes of approaching our tasks and goals if we were to try to think beyond the terms with which we have become so comfortable and to which we have become inured. This was the theme in Chapter 3, and it fits in well here with my final step in questioning what I proposed in Chapter 2 was a sincere call to thinking

What stands on the other side of "teacher"? Is it student? Perhaps pupil? Or learner? Athlete? Language conceals, and at times congeals, aspects of culture; for, like the moraine of a glacier, it slowly pushes along ahead of itself the pithy material churned up from the terrain through which it has passed. In German, for example, the word for student, *der Schüler,* etymologically stands apart from teacher, *der Lehrer,* a word related more closely to the verb for "study," *lernen.* And the English word "learner," by way of the Anglo-Saxon *leornian,* is derived from the same Germanic shared root word. Likewise our word for "teach" comes straight from the Anglo-Saxon, *tæcan.* But the word used for a teacher—to describe someone with special skills, someone who knew the secrets of a craft, who knew how to make and do special things—was *wita,* which came from the verb "to know," *witan.* And so "guide" and "instruct" were both expressed through the word *wissian;* and the adjective used to qualify such a person was *wislic.* Our word "wisdom" remains unchanged from how it was used in Anglo-Saxon times a thousand years ago. But what does wisdom have to do with guiding and instructing, with teaching? In what way is wise teaching guiding? In teaching do teachers guide toward wisdom?

Whether we conceptualize teachers as standing with, or over, or opposed to, students, the fact remains that the one requires the other for its meaning. In this regard we need to consider what are the implications of the premise that the student should come first where instruction is involved. By taking this to heart, coaches—teachers—remain learners themselves even (and especially) when teaching. This is not to say teachers should think of themselves as always being apprentices or that they are inadequate to teach their chosen subject of instruction. Rather it keeps the door open for the teacher to think of herself as someone who still has things to learn, whether about teaching in general or regarding her area of specialization. Also, as was discussed in Chapter 4, it allows for learners, in some significant ways, to be teachers, whether of themselves, of their peers, of their teachers, of administrators, of policy-makers. . . . In this regard, the root word in Hebrew (למד) remains at the core of the words for *teach*, *great scholar*, *learn*, and *student*—no less than for that great compendium of learned teachings, the Talmud.

But what can we learn from this? That the teacher and student sometimes exist in close relation to one another linguistically if not culturally, socially, and academically? While not every teacher is a coach and not every student is in the traditional sense an athlete, still these designations call to mind an effective relationship for conveying and mastering basic skills—and much more besides. Whether we want or deserve to take on the title "coach," we can think of ourselves in this capacity for everyday our students, to some extent, are stretching their proverbial mental-muscles as you draw them out and then lead them along a course of healthy and enriching intellectual development. This gives new meaning to Socrates' claim that one's true capacity for learning can be observed in the gymnasium, for it is here that the teacher can spot at a glance who will be an apt learner and who will be a dull pupil.

What Socrates meant by this, I believe, points us back to three main themes upon which, as this chapter has insisted, lifelong learning depends—especially if it is to be authentic and enduring. First, improvisation; how adeptly and gracefully one responds when confronted by an unfamiliar situation without, as it were, missing a beat (as was mentioned in the opening section of this chapter). Physical activity (and all that comes under the heading of body language) can show the mind's true intentions more readily and obviously than can subtle conversation or written examinations (at least to those attuned to its lexicon and syntax). Second, respect; how readily and openly one honors the spirit of an endeavor in and of itself even, and especially, when it does not count (as was discussed in terms of the salute) [also, see again, FIGURE 4.2, the bottom component). And finally Socrates meant, I think, that the integration of these two aspects, of improvisation and respect, are paramount where the aptitude and desire for lifelong learning are concerned. Seen in this way, improvisation and respect are valid responses to anarchy and education; to the swirling chaos of possibilities that is differentiated and made manageable by virtue of one's having been trained in the best the tradition has to offer—balanced by the power to think and the desire to rebel. But: What to respect, and what to reform, and what to reject outright? Herein lies the challenge each of us must take to heart in our effort to put the needs of each of our students first, so as to teach in such a way that we are more likely to let learning happen.

And this brings us back full circle to the bouting method, for the mark of having taught the student successfully according to this approach means that before too long she will no longer need you to find opportunities to learn (though now your role as mentor, as guide, is really just beginning). She can learn more from applying and doing in bouts what it is you have taught her than by being drilled in yet another closely related technique. In this sense the coach who has taught best is the one who soonest is not required for the student to learn. And so it may be the case in other disciplines as it is in fencing: the teacher teaches most when not teaching. Perhaps this is the ultimate, if paradoxical, lesson to be learned from fencing.

# Conclusion

The student comes first. What comes next is open for discussion. For example, what is to be taught, how to teach it, who should teach it, how to go about assessing what the students are expected to learn and who decides this. But however such issues are settled in the end, the student still needs to come first. In this book, as in my teaching, despite my tendency to revel in my own ingenuity, I have sought, every step of the way, to keep the needs of students foremost in mind.

Education is about students. It is not about programs, mandates, hiring policies, technology budgets, reform packages, or centers for teaching. Students come first. No matter how it might be justified, when students are seen as a means to accomplish this or that end, we lose sight of why teachers are there—to teach. Of course programs must be developed, funded, and administered. Of course studies must be run to chart the relative success of this or that program. Of course funds must be raised to keep everything running. Of course teachers, faculty, and staff must be hired and fired, promoted and transferred, motivated and kept in line. But still, students should come first. If we are driven by anything else, then we are compromising what matters most in education.

Teachers have much to learn. Not only about the content of what they teach, but also about how they are going teach it, whether for the first or the fifth time. Each student provides you, the teacher, with opportunities to remember how you learn best, and to learn something from this. In this respect, teachers need to recognize they are students too. Education is about letting learning happen. And, more specifically, because the student comes first, education is about letting students learn. Despite pressure from above—or from within—teachers are the ultimate guardians of this truth.

177

# Bibliography

> Let people see in what I borrow whether I have known how to choose what would enhance my theme. For I make others say what I cannot say so well, now through the weakness of my language, now through the weakness of my understanding. I do not count my borrowings; I weigh them. And if I had wanted to have them valued by their number, I should have loaded myself with twice as many.
>
> — Montaigne's *Essays*, II.10: 296

Alinksy, Saul. *Rules for Radicals: A Pragmatic Primer for Realistic Radicals*. New York: Vintage Books, 1972.

Abbott, Jacob. *History of Xerxes the Great*. New York: A. L. Burt, n.d.

Arnold, Matthew. "Doing as One Likes," *Culture and Anarchy* [1869], in *Poetry and Criticism of Matthew Arnold*. Edited by A. Dwight Culler. Boston: Houghton Mifflin, 1961.

Bacon, Francis. *Advancement of Learning*. London, 1605.

Bakunin, Michael. *God and the State* [1871]. New York: Dover Publications, 1970.

Bath, Michael. *Speaking Pictures: The Emblem Book in Renaissance Culture*. London and New York: Longman, 1994.

Beguinet, Alex. *Technical Manual*. Compiled for the United States Fencing Association, National Coaching Development Program (revised 1999).

Bellah, Robert N., Richard Madsen, William M. Sullivan, Ann Swindler, and Steven M. Tipton. *Habits of the Heart: Individualism and Commitment in American Life*. 1985; rpt., Berkeley and Los Angeles: University of California Press, 1996.

Bellezza, Francis S. "Mnemonic Devices and Memory Schema," in *Imagery and Related Mnemonic Processes*. Edited by Mark A.

McDaniel and Michael Pressley, pp 34-55. New York: Springer, 1987.

Betti, Claudia, and Teel Sale. *Drawing: A Contemporary Approach.* 4th Edition. Fort Worth: Harcourt Brace, 1980.

Blanchot, Maurice. *L'espace littéraire.* 1955; rpt., Paris: Gallimard, 1993.

Brandt, Richard. *Ethical Theory.* Engelwood Cliffs, N.J.: Prentice-Hall, 1959.

Brooks, Jacqueline and Martin Brooks. *In Search of Understanding: The Case for Constructivist Classrooms.* Alexandria, VA: Association for Curriculum Development, 1993.

Bradford, Vincent. *Taking Foil Groups to the Competitive Level.* Counter Parry Press, 1994.

Burke, James. *The Day the Universe Changed.* Boston and Toronto: Little, Brown and Company, 1985.

Burton, Richard. *The Book of the Sword.* 1884; rpt., New York: Dover, 1987.

Bushnell, Rebecca W. *A Culture of Teaching: Early Modern Humanism in Theory and Practice.* Ithaca and London: Cornell University Press, 1996.

Carruthers, Mary. "Inventional Mnemonics and the Ornaments of Style: The Case of Etymology," *Connotations* 2.2. (1992): 103-114.

Cassirer, Ernst. *The Myth of the State.* New Haven: Yale University Press, 1973.

Cassirer, Ernst, Paul Oskar Kristeller, and John Herman Randall, Jr. *The Renaissance Philosophy of Man.* Chicago and London: University of Chicago Press, 1948.

Chickering, Jr., Howell D. *Beowulf: A Dual-Language Edition.* New York: Doubleday (Anchor Books), 1989.

Crane, R.S. *The Idea of the Humanities and Other Essays Critical and Historical.* Chicago: University of Chicago Press, 1967.

Crump, Galbraith Miller. *The Mystical Design of "Paradise Lost."* Lewisburg, PA: Bucknell University Press, 1975.

Corbett, Margery and Richard Lightbown. *The Comely Frontispiece: The Emblematic Title Page in England, 1550-1660.* London: Routledge & Kegan Paul, 1979.

Deleuze, Gilles and Félix Guattari. *What is Philosophy?* Translated by Hugh Tomlinson and Graham Burchell. New York: Columbia University Press, 1994.

Dewey, John. *Art as Experience*. 1934; rpt., New York: Perigee Books, 1980.

Dressel, P. "Grades: One more Tilt at the Windmill," in *Bulletin*. Edited by A.W. Chickering. Memphis: Memphis State University (Center for the Study of Higher Education), 1983.

Engar, Ann W. Response published in "Looking Backward, Looking Forward: MLA Members Speak," *Publications of the Modern Languages Association* 115, No 7 (December 2000).

Faulkner, William. *Light in August* [1932]. New York: Vintage Books, 1972.

Freire, Paulo and Antonio Faundez. *Learning to Question: A Pedagogy of Liberation*. New York: Continuum, 1989.

Garber, Marjorie, Beatrice Hanssen, and Rebecca L. Walkowitz. *The Turn to Ethics*. New York: Routledge, 2000.

Gardner, Howard. *Frames of Mind*. New York: Basic Books, 1983.

Garret, M., E. Kaidanov, and G. Pezza. *Foil, Saber, and Épée Fencing*. University Park, PA: Pennsylvania State University Press, 1994.

Gaugler, William. *Fencing Terminology*. Laureate Press, 1997.

Giovio, Paolo. *Dialogo dell'imprese militari e amorose*. Lyons, 1559.

Goodman, Paul. *Compulsory Mis-eduction and The Community of Scholars*. New York: Vintage Books, 1964.

Guilford, J. P. "The Three Faces of Intellect," *American Psychologist* 14 (1959): 469-79.

Hegel, George Wilhelm Friedrich. *Aesthetics: Lectures on Fine Art*, Vol. 1[published 1835]. Translated by T. M. Knox. Oxford: Clarendon Press, 1975.

Heidegger, Martin. *Being and Time* [1926]. Translated by Joan Stambaugh. Albany: State University of New York Press, 1996.

———. *History of the Concept of Time: Prolegomena*. Translated by Theodore Kisiel. Bloomington and Indianapolis: Indiana University Press, 1992.

———. "The Origin of the Work of Art" [1935-1936]. Translated by Albert Hofstadter, in *Poetry, Language, Thought*. New York: Harper & Row, 1971.

———. *Paremenides*. Translated by André Schuwer and Richard Rojcewicz. Bloomington and Indianapolis: University of Indiana Press, 1994.

———. *What is Called Thinking?* [1954]. Translated by J. Glenn Gray. New York: Harper & Row, 1968.

Huizinga, Johan. *Homo Ludens: The Play-Element in Culture*. 1944; rpt., Boston: Beacon Press, 1955.

Hulse, Clark. *The Rule of Art: Literature and Painting in the Renaissance*. Chicago and London: University of Chicago Press, 1990.

Jackson, Anita and Jane Stoneback. "The Teaching Learning Puzzle: A Student Perspective," in *Interactive Teaching and Learning*. Edited by Hans Klein. Needham, MA: World Association for Case Method Research and Application, 1997: 311-19.

Jones, David H. *Moral Responsibility in the Holocaust: A Study in the Ethics of Character*. Lanham, Boulder, New York, and Oxford: Rowman & Littlefield, 1999.

Kant, Immanuel. *Critique of Judgment* [1790]. Translated by Werner S. Pluhar. Indianapolis: Hackett, 1987.

Kinney, Arthur F. *John Skelton, Priest as Poet: Seasons of Discovery*. Chapel Hill and London: University of North Carolina Press, 1987.

Kohn, Alfie. *The Case Against Standardized Testing: Raising the Scores, Ruining the Schools*. Westport: Heinemann, 2000.

Kropotkin, Peter. *Act for Yourselves: Articles from "Freedom"* [1886-1907]. Edited by Nicolas Walter and Heiner Becker. London: Freedom Press, 1988.

Kropotkin, Peter. *"The Conquest of Bread* [1892]*" and Other Writings*. Edited by Marshall Shatz. Cambridge: Cambridge University Press, 1995.

Lindley, Daniel A. *"This Rough Magic": The Life of Teaching*. Westport, CT: Bergin & Garvey, 1993.

Longus, *Daphnis and Chloe*. Translated by Paul Turner. 1956; rpt., Penguin, 1989.

Mager, Robert F. *Preparing Instructional Objectives*. Second edition. Belmont, CA: Fearon Publishers, Inc. 1975.

Mandelbaum, Allen. *The Divine Comedy of Dante Alighieri: Inferno*. Drawings by Barry Moser. Toronto, New York, London: Bantam Books, 1988.

Marcuse, Herbert. *The Aesthetic Dimension: Toward a Critique of Marxist Aesthetics*. Boston: Beacon Press, 1978.

Margulies, Nancy. *Mapping Inner Space*. Tucson: Zephyr Press, 1991.

Martin, Daniel. "Pour une lecture mnémonique des *Essais*: une image et un lieu" in *Bulletin de la Société des Amis de Montaigne*, 5th series, nos. 31-32 (1979): 51-58.

———. *Le Triptyque des "Essais" de Montaigne*. Tours: A.-G. Nizet, 1996.

McLeod, Jay. *Ain't No Makin' It: Leveled Aspirations in a Low-income Neighborhood*. Boulder: Westview Press, 1987.

Micahnik, Dave. "Vox Populi," compiled by Robert Block, *American Fencing* 50. No. 4 (Winter, 2001): 10-11.

Montaigne, Michel de. *Essays*. Translated by Donald Frame. 1943; rpt., Palo Alto: Stanford University Press, 1965.

Milton, Ohmer, Howard R. Pollio, and James A. Eison. *Making Sense of College Grades*. San Francisco: Jossey-Bass, 1986.

Nänny, Max. "Chiastic Structures in Literature: Some Forms and Functions" in *The Structure of Texts*. Edited by Udo Fries. Tübingen: Gunter Narr, 1987: 75-97.

Nietzsche, Friedrich. *The Birth of Tragedy and the Genealogy of Morals*. New York: Doubleday, 1956.

———. "On the Uses and Disadvantages of History for Life" [1874]. *Untimely Meditations*. Translated by R. J. Holingdale. Cambridge: Cambridge University Press 1999.

———. *Thus Spoke Zarathustra* [1884]. Translated by Walter Kaufman. Penguin Books, 1978.

———. *The Will to Power*. Translated by Walter Kaufman and R. J. Hollingdale. New York: Vintage Books, 1968.

Ohanian, Susan. *One size fits few: The Folly of Educational Standards*. Portsmouth, N.H.: Heinemann, 1999.

Panofsky, Erwin. *Meaning in the Visual Arts*. Chicago: University of Chicago Press, 1955.

Parks, Sharon Daloz. "Is it too late? Young Adults and the Formation of Professional Ethics" in *Can Ethics be Taught?* Edited by Thomas Piper, Mary C. Gentile, and Sharon Daloz Parks. Boston: Harvard Business School, 1993: 13-72.

Piper, Thomas R. Piper. "A Program for Management Education" in *Can Ethics be Taught?* Edited by Thomas Piper, Mary C. Gentile, and Sharon Daloz Parks. Boston: Harvard Business School, 1993: 117-160.

Plutarch. *Moralia* [in sixteen volumes]. Vol. 1. Translated by Frank Cole Babbitt. Loeb Classical Library. Cambridge: Harvard University Press. 1927; rpt., 1986.

Raymond, G.L. *The Representative Significance of Form*. Putnam's Sons, 1909.

Rorty, Richard. *Contingency, Irony, and Solidarity*. Cambridge, 1989.

Rosovsky, Henry. *The University: An Owner's Manual*. New York: W.W. Norton, 1990.

Ross, Alexander. *The Historie of the World, Part II* . London, 1652.

Rossellius, G. *Thesaurus Artificiosae Memoriae*. Venice, 1579.

Røstvig, Maren-Sofie. *Configurations: A Topomorphical Approach to Renaissance Poetry*. Oslo Copenhagen-Stockholm: Scandinavian University Presses, 1994.

Rushton, David. Unpublished "Reflective Essay," 1998.

Russell, Bertrand. *Sceptical Essays*. 1929; rpt., London: Routledge, 1977.

Sallis, John. *Stone*. Bloomington and Indianapolis: University of Indiana Press, 1994.

————. *Double Truth*. Albany: State University of New York Press, 1995.

Schneider, Alison. "Insubordination and Intimidation Signal the End of Decorum in Many Classrooms" in *The Chronicle of Higher Education*. March 27, 1998.

Schon, D. *The Reflective Process*. Basic Books, 1983.

Selman, Matthew, Jerry Selman, Henry Cory, and Victor Selman. "Transformational Protocols for Millennium-3," *Proceedings of the International Conference for Innovation in Higher Education* (1998).

Skinner, Quentin and Russell Price. *The Prince*. Cambridge: Cambridge University Press, 1989.

Slama, Patricia. "The Myth of the Expert," in *Interactive Teaching and Learning*. Edited by Hans Klein. Needham, MA: World Association for Case Method Research and Application, 1997: 377-81.

Smith, Page. *Killing the Spirit: Higher Education in America*. New York: Penguin Books, 1990.

Solomon, Robert and Jon Solomon. *Up the University: Re-Creating Higher Education in America*. Reading, MA: Addison-Wesley, 1993.

Sylvester, Richard S. *English Sixteenth-Century Verse*. New York: W.W. Norton, 1984.

Ueshiba, Morihei. *The Art of Peace [Aikido]*. Boston and London: Shambhala, 1992.

Vaughan, Aislinn. Unpublished "Reflective Essay," 1998.

Yates, Frances. *The Art of Memory*. 1966; rpt., Penguin Books, 1978.

\* \* \* \* \*

Æghwæþres sceal
scearp scyld-wiga     gescad witan,
worda ond worca,     se þe wel þenceð.

[A keen-witted shield-bearer
who thinks things out carefully     must know the distinction
between words and deeds,     keep the difference clear.]

— *Beowulf*, lines 287-89 (Chickering, Jr., 1989: 64-65)

EDUCATION & Ⓐnarchy — At a glance

**Introduction**

**Chapter 1. Classroom Capers**
    I.   Grounding
    II.  Five Main Types
        1.  Tagging
        2.  Memory Grids
        3.  Mind Mapping
        4.  Magic Circles
        5.  Speaking Pictures
    III. Moving On

**Chapter 2.  Letting Learning Happen**
    I.   Manifesto
    II.  Demonstration
        1.  Plan Of Study
            1$^{st}$ Unit: Macrocosm & Microcosm
            2$^{nd}$ Unit: Discovery Of The Self
            3$^{rd}$ Unit: The Will To Power
            4$^{th}$ Unit: World Of Words
        2.  Motto, Expectations, And Key Questions
    III. Credo

**Chapter 3.  Speaking Of Teaching**
**Chapter 4.  What Can Be Taught**
    I.   Preamble
    II.  Three Possibilities
        1.  Literature And Human Values
        2.  Educating The Princes
        3.  Books With Bill
            *Socrates/Plato*
            *Cervantes*
            *Machiavelli*
    III. Drawing The Line

**Chapter 5:  The Sword Of Truth**
    I.   Introduction
    II.  The Way Of The Sword
        1.  Salute
        2.  On Guard
        3.  Preparations
            *Body Movements*
            *Blade Actions*
        4.  Offensive
            *Attacks*
            *Ripostes*
            *Varied Offensive*
        5.  Defensive
            *Evasions*
            *Parries*
        6.  Counter-Offensive
    III.  Lessons Learned From Fencing

**Conclusion**

# About the Author

After a decade of university teaching Bill Engel became a Visiting Scholar at Harvard's Philosophy of Education Research Center. He continues to teach in a variety of venues, but where he does not have to grade papers. The author welcomes suggestions about how this book can be improved for future editions: Bill@Engelwood.net.